Sew

Classic Clothes

for Girls

Sew
CLASSIC CLOTHES
for Girls

20
GIRLS' DRESSES, OUTFITS
and ACCESSORIES
from the COTTAGE MAMA

Lindsay Wilkes

KP CRAFT
CINCINNATI, OHIO

Meet the Author

Lindsay Wilkes is the owner and designer of The Cottage Mama (www.thecottagemama.com), a boutique children's clothing and sewing pattern company, and the writer behind the popular sewing and crafting blog, The Cottage Mama (www.thecottagemama.com/blog). She is known for her use of contemporary printed designer cotton fabric, her love of unique trims, timeless style and vintage details. Lindsay enjoys sewing, cooking, crafting and all things domestic. She resides in Chicago, Illinois, with her husband and three young children.

Website: www.thecottagemama.com
Blog: www.thecottagemama.com/blog
Facebook: www.facebook.com/thecottagemama
Twitter: www.twitter.com/thecottagemama
Pinterest: www.pinterest.com/thecottagemama
E-mail: thecottagemama@gmail.com

Meet the Photographer

Amy Tripple is an award-winning child and family photographer whose work has been featured in *Adoptive Families*, *The Cute Kid*, *Panama America*, and NAPCP (National Association of Professional Child Photographers) publications. Her fresh, natural approach to photography allows her subjects' personalities to shine through her images. Amy resides in Downers Grove, Illinois with her husband and three beautiful children.

Website: www.amytripplephotography.com

This book is dedicated to my children, Savannah Rose,
Matilda Jane and Caspian Finn,
the three best things I have ever created.

CONTENTS

INTRODUCTION

I'm a classic, traditional girl at heart. I've always had a fondness for the styles of the 1930s, 40s and 50s. While I adore the adult fashions from these eras, I have a true soft spot in my heart for the sweet and innocent look of vintage children's fashions. Those were simpler times—a time when little girls truly dressed like little girls.

In earlier days, our grandparents and great-grandparents made clothing for their children out of necessity. It was far less expensive to buy a yard of fabric and make a dress than it was to head to the store and buy one. Obviously, that is not the case today. With much of our clothing being manufactured overseas, the cost of store-bought clothing is more affordable. But, my guess is that if you're reading this book, then you see the value, beauty and uniqueness of handmade clothing.

I grew up with a mom who sewed. I fondly remember wearing handmade costumes to every party and costume parade. I always had the best costume in class; they were truly little works of art. Year after year my friends would ask me where I got my costume, and I was so proud to tell them that my mom had actually made it for me. This was during the 1980s, a time when the art of handmade was pushed slightly to the wayside as many women found themselves working full-time and, thus, relying on convenience items.

Three decades later, handmade items have made a big comeback. While I don't know exactly why, I think we're all longing for simpler times. Our lives have become so hectic, and sewing offers us an opportunity to slow down. It appears that many women are once again embracing the value of handmade items and realizing that placing an emphasis on this aspect of their home lives is a worthwhile endeavor.

Sewing children's clothing is a wonderful creative outlet, and with so many gorgeous fabrics and trims on the market today, it's easy to create beautiful, one-of-a-kind garments. Sometimes it's as much fun for a mother or grandmother to see their little one wearing the clothing as it is for the child to wear it! It's also a great way to show your children just how much you care about them. The look on a child's face when they put on a handmade garment is priceless. Every morning as my two little girls get dressed, they ask me, "Mama, did you make this for me?" When I am able to respond with a yes, they get the biggest smile on their faces and shower me with thanks. They are thrilled to pieces that I took the time to create a handmade article of clothing especially for them. Besides, my girls will only be little for such a short period of time, and I want to preserve their childhood for as long as possible. One of the ways I can do that is through the clothing that I sew for them.

I have created the core patterns in this book to be used as a full collection. I wanted to offer you a way to make an entire wardrobe that can be mixed and matched to create many unique and different looks for your little one. Layered with solid, colorful long- and short-sleeved t-shirts, tights and jeans, this collection will be versatile enough for all seasons.

If you are going to take the time to sew for your little lady, take the time to make each piece truly special and with quality materials. Select gorgeous fabrics, unique trims and special buttons. Each pattern comes with several different design variations, and once you learn how to construct the main pattern, you will be able to get creative with the many different design ideas offered here.

I want you to get excited about sewing for your little ones. Yes, there are tips and tricks that will give your garments a more professional look, but there are no hard and fast rules. Just have fun! If you find a shortcut that works for you, then go with it. This is your chance to make something for your little girl that she will truly cherish. We may not be on this earth forever, but through sewing, we can leave behind little bits of sewn love.

Happy Sewing,
Lindsay Wilkes

Getting Started

THERE ARE MANY TIPS, TOOLS AND TECHNIQUES that can start off your garment sewing on the right foot. Fabric selection, fabric pairing and trim selection can truly take your garments from ordinary to extraordinary. In this section, I will share some of the ideas, techniques and tools I use when creating one-of-a-kind pieces for little ones. Many of the tools found in the following pages are ones that I find helpful in sewing children's clothing. While all of them are not "must-haves," some of them might make your life easier. Let's get sewing!

FABRIC SELECTION

A large part of what makes a garment unique is the fabric selection. The same pattern in different fabrics will result in two entirely different looks. Whether it's a mix of printed cottons or different textured fabrics, fabric selection is key to creating unique, quality garments.

For children's clothing, you can't go wrong with high-quality 100-percent woven cotton. There are certainly different grades of cotton fabrics on the market, and one of the easiest ways to tell the difference between high- and low-quality fabric is to feel or *hand* them. The hand of a fabric is just what it sounds like: the feel and drape.

The more you get into sewing, the more you will come to know which manufacturers are producing fabrics with a hand that is right for you and your child. Obviously, if you're just starting out, some trial and error will be involved. A lesser-quality fabric tends to feel stiff and scratchy, the dyes often bleed, and it can shrink quite a bit. Better-quality fabrics tend to be soft and smooth with minimal to no dye bleeding.

Make It Just Sew: Selecting Fabric

There are two major factors to consider when selecting fabric for children's garments:

- ☺ Are the clothes intended to be play clothes, special occasion wear or school clothes?

- ☺ What season will your child be wearing the garment?

The fabric type can drastically change the look and feel of the garment, almost as much as the actual print or design of the fabric. There are many different fabrics to choose from when sewing for children, but here is a selection of fabrics that are very suitable to children's wear:

100-percent woven cotton | Chambray
Lined eyelet | Denim | Twill | Batiste | Seersucker
Soft wool | Corduroy | Linen | Cotton/linen blend
Cotton knit | Dobby cotton | Velvet | Velveteen

PAIRING PATTERNED FABRICS

Pairing patterned fabrics might be a bit challenging at first, but once you get the hang of it, you may find it the most fun, creative part of sewing. I know I do!

Fabric selection can make or break a garment. On one hand, if the fabrics are paired properly, they can create a definite "wow" statement; if paired incorrectly, they can make the garment look, well ... wrong. Luckily, today's quilting fabric designers make coordinating fabrics fairly simple by offering complementary fabrics that are designed to go together. Within a designer's collection are typically various *color ways*, or fabrics that are similar in color and tone. However, just because a fabric coordinates with another doesn't mean it's going to work well for a child's garment.

The key to successfully combining patterned fabrics is to properly select and place fabrics of varying scales. A good rule of thumb is to never have more than one large-scale print per garment. A child's garment is fairly small and too many large prints will overwhelm the look. However, this doesn't mean you should use only small-scale prints either. Sometimes too many small-scale prints can result in a bland or dated look.

When coordinating three patterned fabrics, try to select one large print, one medium print and a small print, or a medium print and two small prints. If you are combining more than three fabrics, never select more than one large print and one medium print; the rest should be small scale and/or solid colors.

A great way to help select fabrics is to focus on the colors. Look closely at the main print and pull out the individual colors. You will have a main focus color and several coordinating accent colors. Sometimes focusing on the accent colors can really help during this process. The accent colors seem to go somewhat unnoticed, but when brought out with coordinating prints (and trims), these colors can really create a stunning look. After you have narrowed in on a couple colors, go to your local fabric shop or dig into your fabric stash and play around. Get out fabrics and lay them on top of one another. How does the combination make you feel? Does it work for you? Does it give you the feeling you want? You are going to be your best judge. If you think that things don't look right, then pull out more

fabrics. Mix and match until you have a coordinated look that you love.

Consider bringing in pattern prints such as gingham, polka dots, stripes, damask, or small-scale florals as accent fabrics. You can always play it safe with solids, and sometimes that can be the best choice, but I encourage you to challenge yourself to create a look from all patterned fabrics. I think you'll truly surprise yourself with the amazing garments you can create.

TRIMS AND EMBELLISHMENTS

Trims are a great way to help tie fabrics together and add a uniqueness to your garments. Adding piping into a seam can break up two different patterned fabrics and ultimately help them work together. If there is a color you are trying to highlight in a certain fabric, selecting a trim in that color can be a great way to help draw focus and emphasize that specific color.

Great sources for unique, one-of-a-kind trims are antique stores, flea markets and estate sales. This is where you can happen upon a treasure trove of trims and embellishments that you may not be able to find anywhere else. Just make sure to check the composition of the trims if they come in the packaging. If you're not sure about a trim, it's a good idea to test out a little piece in a load of laundry. It's never fun to work really hard on a beautiful garment only to have the piece not wash well. Trust me, I've been there.

If you're not up for a treasure hunt in antique stores or flea markets, there are many wonderful local shops and online resources for purchasing quality trims.

You can add rickrack, piping, loopy trim and many more trim options into or on top of most seams. For rickrack trim, position the center of the trim in the seam allowance of the garment; this will cause the rickrack to poke through with a sort of scalloped edge in the seam. Depending on the size of the trim, sometimes you can just line up the edge of the rickrack with the

edge of the garment, but you will have to measure your trim to see if you will need to adjust the placement. You will learn more about inserting piping into seams later in the book.

When you are thinking of adding trim to a garment, consider layering trims for a more dramatic look. Add ribbon on top of rickrack, or add piping behind a piece of woven trim. You'll hear me say this many times in this book, but get creative!

PATTERNS AND SIZE SELECTIONS

All of the patterns, layout cutting diagrams and yardage requirements for the book are contained on the CD in PDF form. Having all of the patterns on CD allows you to use the patterns time and time again without having to trace them.

To use the PDF pattern disk, insert the disk into your computer, select your desired garment and print it off on your home printer. Check the 2" (5cm) box to make sure you have printed the patterns at the proper scale. If not, check your printer and make sure you don't have any scaling settings selected. You do not want scaling.

Tape the pattern pieces together according to the pattern markings. Read all the information on each pattern piece, and follow the Layout Sheet to pin your pattern pieces to your fabric(s). Transfer any markings from the pattern pieces to your fabric. Then cut out your desired size and begin your project.

In order to select the proper pattern sizing, measure your child beforehand if possible. Use a soft tailor's ruler to measure the child's height, chest and waist.

Please use the sizing chart shown here when selecting the proper garment size for your child. All designs in this book were created using these measurements.

Size	Height	Weight (lbs)	Waist/Chest/Inseam
12 Months	29"–31" (74cm–79cm)	22–27	19½"/20"/10½" (50cm/51cm/27cm)
2T	33"–36" (84cm–91cm)	30–32	20¼"/22"/13" (51cm/56cm/33cm)
4	39"–42" (99cm–107cm)	35–41	21¼"/24"/16" (54cm/61cm/41cm)
6	45"–48" (114cm–122cm)	46–51	22½"/26"/19½" (57cm/66cm/50cm)
8	51"–54" (130cm–137cm)	57–66	23¾"/28"/23" (60cm/71cm/58cm)
10	55"–58" (140cm–147cm)	76–85	25"/29"–30"/25¼" (64cm/74cm–76cm/64cm)

Make It Just Sew: Before You Begin Sewing

- ☺ Please read all pattern instructions thoroughly before beginning.

- ☺ All seam allowances are ½" (13mm) unless otherwise noted.

- ☺ Prewash and press all fabrics and trims prior to garment construction. This will eliminate any shrinkage as well as dye bleeding.

- ☺ Always pin or weight down pattern pieces when cutting to avoid any shifting that may occur.

- ☺ Transfer all pattern markings onto fabric using a water-soluble fabric marking pen.

- ☺ When working with pants, shorts or knickers patterns, always mark the front and the back of the pants to avoid confusion.

- ☺ Always press your seams as you go to ensure a professional-looking garment.

TOOLS OF THE TRADE

CUTTING AND PRESSING

Dressmakers' shears (a): A nice pair of shears reserved for your sewing is a must! Do not let your family use these scissors for regular tasks—keep them for sewing only so they remain sharp. Cutting paper with your shears will dull the blades.

Iron: If there is one takeaway from this book, I hope you learn the importance of pressing while sewing. It's almost as important as the sewing itself! If you do not press as you go, you will end up with an unprofessional, sloppy-looking garment. It is during pressing that a garment truly takes its shape, so whatever you do, do not skip pressing.

Pinking shears (b): Pinking shears are often used to cut the raw edges of fabric so it doesn't fray. If you don't have the time to zigzag stitch the edge of your fabric or you don't have a serger, you can use pinking shears to prevent the fabrics from fraying on the raw edges. Pinking shears are also great for trimming seams around curves so that they lay flat.

Rotary cutter (c) and mat: I like to use a rotary cutter to cut out garment patterns. Simply weight down the pattern pieces with pattern weights and cut around them with a rotary cutter. If you have trouble cutting around curves, try using a tiny rotary cutter to work around them. A rotary cutter is also great for cutting straight lines, custom piping, ruffles and sashes.

If you want to use a rotary cutter, you will need a rotary cutting mat. These mats come in all different sizes, but for garment sewing, you should consider purchasing one that is the size of a full yard of fabric. The mat will protect your hard surfaces from the blade.

Scissors (d): A small pair of scissors is wonderful when you are working on hand-sewing or trimming threads from garments. **Appliqué scissors (e)** are also handy. These curved scissors are perfect for cutting around hand- or machine-appliqué designs.

Seam ripper (f): Unfortunately, some days your seam ripper and you will be inseparable. It happens to the best of us.

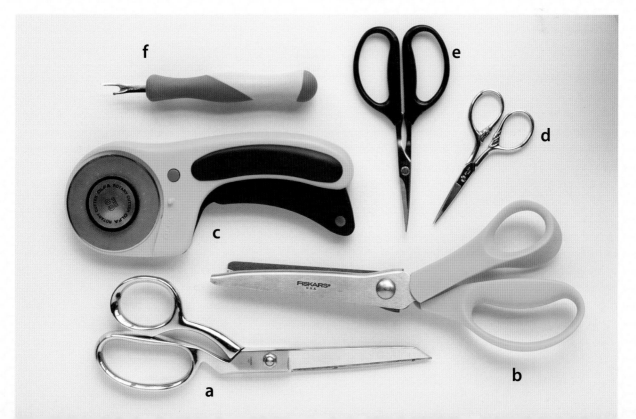

MACHINES AND ACCESSORIES

Buttonhole foot (g): Buttonholes can be scary, but they aren't if you have a buttonhole foot. If your machine did not come with one, go purchase one. It will be worth every penny!

Machine sewing needles (h): Make sure you use the proper needle for your fabric. There are specific needles designed just for use with denim or heavier fabrics, knit fabrics, silk, etc. A universal 80/12 needle is fine for quilting weight cotton; however, if you want to make the coat or pants in a heavier-weight fabric, switch to a denim needle.

Piping foot: A piping foot is great to have in your collection if you are sewing piping into garments on a regular basis. This foot is specifically designed with a groove that allows the cording to feed under the foot smoothly.

Ruffler foot (i): If you plan to sew a lot of ruffles, you should definitely consider investing in a ruffler foot. It snaps onto your sewing machine and makes beautiful and evenly spaced ruffles in no time flat. There are rufflers designed for each specific sewing machine, and there are also generic rufflers on the market. I would suggest purchasing the one that is made for your specific sewing machine.

Serger: While none of the patterns in this book require a serger, it is a nice tool to have around if you plan to really get into garment sewing. A serger typically has 3–4 threads that add a reinforced seam and an edge free of frayed fabric. The durability a serged seam gives a garment is wonderful for children's clothing.

Serger gathering foot (j): If you have a serger, a gathering foot is invaluable. The gathering foot gathers one piece of fabric, attaches it to another and serges the edge all at one time. Talk about a triple-duty foot! Again, not a "must-have," but it's a tool that will have you asking, "Where have you been my whole life?".

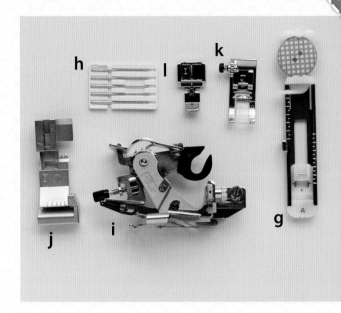

Sewing machine: There are many different sewing machines on the market today. If you're just starting out, you don't need anything fancy. A basic entry-level machine that will do a straight stitch and a zigzag stitch is perfectly fine. The standard **presser foot (k)** that comes with your machine will get you started. If you want to make your life easier, a one-step buttonhole feature is also nice. As you advance, you might consider a fancier machine, as the ability to use different decorative stitches and machine embroidery can certainly take your sewing to the next level.

Thread: For the purposes of the patterns in this book, you should only use polyester threads, as they are strong and durable. Select a thread that matches your garment. If you can't find something exact, you are better off selecting a lighter color thread than a darker thread, as lighter ones tend to blend better. If you plan to add any embroidery, follow your machine's instructions to choose the appropriate thread.

Zipper foot (l): There are no zippers included in the patterns in this book, but a zipper foot is handy for sewing piping into garments (although not necessary). Most machines come with one, but if yours didn't, look into purchasing one.

MEASURING, MARKING AND PINNING

Fabric marking pen (m): There are several different fabric marking pens on the market. I prefer the type that wash out with water, but there are some that will also disappear after a certain amount of time. I prefer a marking pen over chalk because I find them to be more accurate and the marks won't rub off. But again, choose what works for you.

Fray Check (n): Fray Check is a product you can use to finish any edge you don't want to unravel. It's a great product to use on the end of ribbons that have been cut. You can also use it after you have cut through your buttonholes to make sure they stay fray free. Use it on the beginning and ending of serged stitching to prevent unraveling. There are other anti-fray products on the market, but whatever brand you choose, it's a good product to have on hand.

Hand-sewing needle: There are some things that just need to be sewn by hand, like buttons or small details, so get yourself a set of sharp hand-sewing needles. Also, if you would like to add any hand embroidery to your garments, make sure you purchase the appropriate hand-embroidery needles as well.

Hem gauge (o): A hem gauge is one of those tools that I don't know how people sew without. It's an easy way to measure your button, strap and trim placement, as well as hems or casings.

Pattern weights (p): Pattern weights are great for holding patterns in place while you cut them out with a rotary cutter. There are many different commercial brands sold in stores, but you can make your own by picking up some large metal washers at your local hardware store. Keep fifteen to twenty on hand for pattern cutting.

Piping tool: There are several piping tools on the market. Basically, these tools help you cut your piping to allow

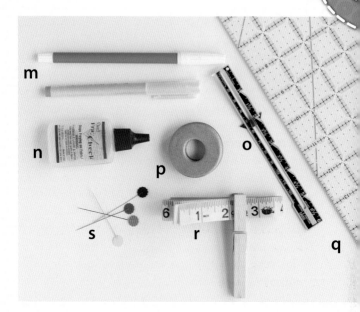

for the proper seam allowance for the garment you are sewing. For example, if you are sewing a garment using a ¼" (6mm) seam allowance, you can use your piping tool to cut the raw edge down to ¼" (6mm) to ensure you are completely accurate when inserting it into a seam.

Quilting ruler (q): A quilting ruler for garments? Yes! It's just a great tool to have for cutting precise, straight lines. It can be used to cut rectangles for ruffles, and it makes easy work of cutting bias strips. It's also wonderful for squaring up directional fabric to make sure everything is straight prior to cutting out your patterns.

Soft tape measure (r): You will use this a lot when measuring your children—a necessity to make sure you get an accurate fit.

Straight pins (s): Pinning is very important in sewing. The type of pins you choose to use is entirely up to you. A glass head pin is nice because you can iron on top of it without melting the head; however, a pin with a larger head will be easier to see while you sew. Personally, I like flower head pins because they are a nice length, easy to see and really cute!

SPECIALTY TOOLS

Bias tape maker (t): There are several different size bias tape-making tools that can be used with your iron, allowing you to customize bias tape to your project. Use them to make single-fold bias tape, then fold and iron the fabric strips in half to make double-fold bias tape. Several patterns in this book call for bias tape; if you plan to make your own, make your life easier and pick up one of these tools. There are also bias tape-making machines, so feel free to check those out as well.

Bodkin (u): A bodkin is a little metal tool that is used for threading. Attach it to the end of a piece of elastic or ribbon and move it through a casing for threading. You could also use a safety pin; however, the long, narrow length of a bodkin can be very handy.

Cording (v): If you plan to make your own piping, you will need to purchase cotton cording to use as the filler. For children's garments, you should look for something small, such as size 9 mini cotton cording. You can use any size you like, depending on how you like your piping to appear on your garment.

Point turner (w): A point turner is great for pushing out corners; however, if you don't have one, a chopstick or dull pencil will work just fine.

Skinny loop turner (x): This is the perfect tool for turning skinny tubes, such as spaghetti bias or lacing.

Tube turners (y): Tube turners are a "must have" if you plan to sew for little girls. They make turning sashes, spaghetti bias, straps and more a cinch!

Wash-A-Way Wonder Tape (z): I use this to secure trims to fabric prior to sewing. It is a double-sided sticky tape that washes away after it goes through the laundry. Apply one sticky side to the wrong side of your trim, then peel off the paper, stick the trim where you would like it, and sew in place. Wonder Tape doesn't gum up your needle, so it's safe to sew right through it.

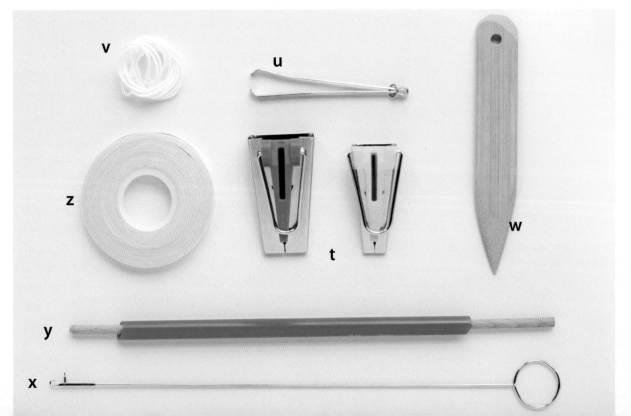

FINISHING TOUCHES

Clothing labels (aa): Even if you aren't selling garments, it is fun to have your own clothing labels to add to your children's garments. You can purchase woven or printed labels at very reasonable prices. Check online for companies that sell custom clothing labels, or consider using a company like Spoonflower.com to have a piece of fabric made with your label/name printed repeatedly. Cut out your label and sew it into your child's garment. The options are endless, but make sure you label your work in some manner. It seems like quilters are really great about labeling their creations, so why shouldn't those that sew garments label their little works of art?

Think about how special it will be for your daughter or granddaughter to hand down a piece of clothing with your label on it thirty years from now!

Covered button kit (bb): Making fabric-covered buttons is very simple if you have one of these inexpensive covered button kits. Covered buttons are a wonderful detail to add to children's clothing.

Yo-yo makers (cc): These tools make really fast work of constructing these vintage embellishments. They come in all shapes and sizes and are very simple to use.

aa

cc

bb

TECHNIQUES

APPLYING BIAS TAPE

Bias tape is a narrow piece of fabric that is cut on the bias (45-degree angle to straight of grain), making it stretchier than fabric cut straight across the grain. Because of its stretchiness, bias tape works great for encasing raw, curved edges.

Readymade bias tape can be purchased in the notions section of your local fabric store. These days, most bias tape comes in basic, solid colors. However, I prefer to make my own bias tape because I can control the quality of the material I'm using, and I can make the tape coordinate with the look of the garment. You may also find vintage bias tape in all sorts of different fun patterns at thrift stores and flea markets.

There are two different types of bias tape available in varying widths: single-fold and double-fold. Single-fold bias tape has two sides folded inwards (one fold is slightly larger than the other), and it is not folded down the center. Double-fold bias tape is basically single-fold bias tape, but folded in half again lengthwise. Double-fold will encase an entire raw edge with bias on either side of the raw edge. Single-fold will allow you to finish a raw edge by folding it toward the inside of a garment, but generally you will not see any bias tape on the exterior of the garment.

There are several garments in this book that require you to use bias tape/binding to finish an edge. Before you apply double-fold bias tape, open up your tape. If you look very closely, you will see that one side has a larger fold than the other. This is a very important detail to notice before you sew on your bias tape.

1 Open up the fold on the narrower side completely. Line up the raw edge of the garment with the raw edge of the bias tape, right sides together. Pin the bias tape in place.

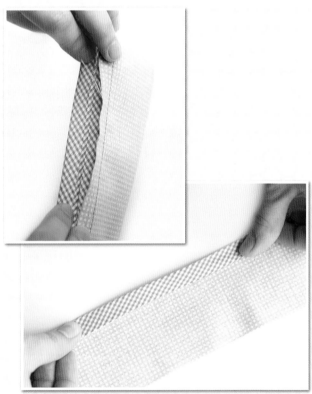

2 Stitch in the fold along the raw edge of both the bias tape and the garment. You are sewing on the right side of the garment. Then fold your bias tape over to the other side (wrong side of the garment).

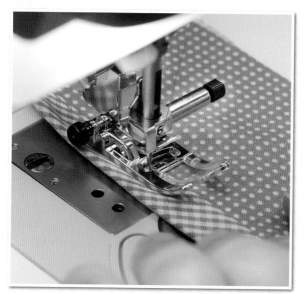

3 Stitch as close to the edge of the bias tape as possible on the right side of the garment. Stitching on this side will ensure that you will catch the larger fold (on the wrong side). Just to clarify, you stitched your original line of stitching on the right side of the garment, and you are doing your second set of stitching on the same side (right side) of the garment.

If you would prefer to see no stitching on the bias tape on the exterior of the garment, when you fold the bias tape over to the wrong side of the garment, use a slipstitch or whipstitch to hand-sew the bias tape to the wrong side. In this case, you will sew your first row of machine stitches on the right side of the garment, fold over the bias tape and sew your second set of hand stitches on the wrong side of the garment.

4 You're finished! The raw edge is completely encased with the bias tape.

- -

Make It Just Sew: Making Bias Facing

Single-fold bias tape works very similarly to double-fold. The only difference is that when you fold your bias tape to the wrong side of the garment, there will be no bias tape showing on the right side of the garment. Instead you will just see a line of stitching on the fabric where you have sewn your single-fold bias tape to the wrong side of the garment.

- -

MAKING YOUR OWN BIAS TAPE

If you really want to add a custom look to your garments, make your own custom bias tape from coordinating fabric. Personally, I prefer custom-made bias tape because I can control the quality of the fabric used to make the bias tape. Most store-bought bias tape is made from a polyester/cotton blend fabric, but by making your own, you can use gorgeous, high-quality quilting cotton or other fabric.

Making your own custom bias tape is also a great way to add a special touch to your children's garments or to incorporate another coordinating fabric print into your design.

There are many different ways to make bias tape, but we are going to focus on the most simplistic technique because we don't need a lot of bias tape yardage.

To make your own bias tape, you will need a rotary cutter, cutting mat, quilting ruler and a 12" × 12" (30cm × 30cm) square of fabric, or add more fabric if you need additional yardage of bias tape.

- -

Make It Just Sew: Bias Strip Width

To determine the width of your bias strips, you will need to multiply the finished binding width by 4. For instance, if you want ½" (13mm) bias tape, you will cut 2" (5cm) strips.

- -

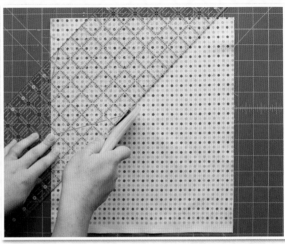

1 You will need to cut the strips on the bias, meaning in the direction of the fabric that has the most stretch. To find the bias, look for the selvage of the fabric. The selvages are the two sides of the fabric that are not cut and don't fray (usually they have the name of the fabric manufacturer listed there). Cut your square of fabric so the sides of the square run parallel and perpendicular to the selvage edges. Lay the fabric in front of you with the selvage edge at the bottom of the square.

2 Cut strips of fabric at a 45-degree angle to the fabric selvage using the markings on your quilting ruler or cutting mat for reference.

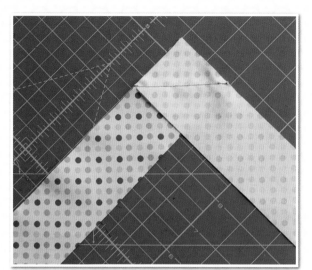

3 To join the bias strips together, square off the ends of two bias strips. Place them on top of one another at a 90-degree angle, right sides together. Stitch the two strips together on a diagonal as shown.

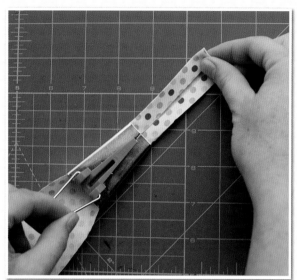

5 With the wrong side up, feed the point of the fabric into the bias tape maker, using a straight pin to pull the fabric through. Use your iron to press the bias tape as it comes through the bias tape maker.

If you don't have a bias tape maker, fold and press the bias strip in half lengthwise, wrong sides together. Unfold the strip. Now fold in both long sides of the strips so they meet in the middle at the previously pressed seam and press.

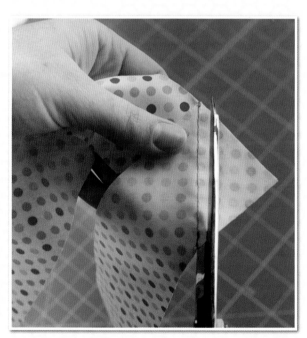

4 Trim the excess fabric, leaving an approximate ½" (13mm) seam allowance. Press the seam open and trim off any pieces that overhang the edges. Continue to join strips until you have reached your desired length of bias tape.

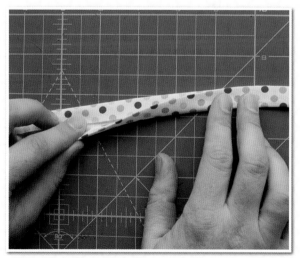

6 To make double-fold bias tape, fold the bias tape in half lengthwise again and press.

INSERTING PIPING

Piping is a narrow piece of fabric, cut on the bias, which encases a piece of cording. Make your own piping or buy premade piping in the notions section of your local fabric store. I think piping is one of the sweetest, most professional details you can add to children's clothing. It makes a somewhat ordinary piece of clothing into something extraordinary.

Piping can be inserted into any seam. Whether you want to add a little piping detail in a collar, waistband or armhole, the options are endless. There are many different colors and sizes of piping that you can purchase premade in the notions section of your local sewing store, but did you know that you can make your own?

If you want to make your life really easy when it comes to inserting piping, get yourself some Wash-A-Way Wonder Tape. In order to sew piping, you do not need Wonder Tape, it's just a nice product to have on hand. You can find Wonder Tape in the notions section of your local fabric store. Wonder Tape can be easily sewn through and will not gum up your needle (most other tapes will mess up your needle). It disappears after washing, too. So, if you are trying to hold something in place and would rather not use pins, Wonder Tape is a great option. In addition to pins, you can also use a glue basting stick to hold piping and trims in place.

2 Align the raw edges of the piping with the raw edge of the fabric with right side up. If you are not using Wonder Tape, pin or baste your piping in place.

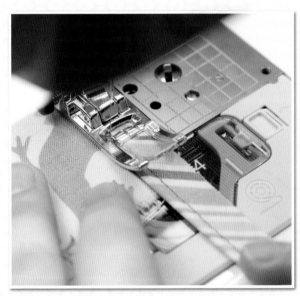

3 Stitch slightly to the left of your original piping stitching. Make sure you stitch to the left, otherwise the original stitching will show through when you turn your garment.

1 Apply Wonder Tape to the side of the piping that will be next to the fabric. After you have applied one side of the tape to the piping, remove the paper backing.

4 With right sides together, match the raw edges and pin the piped piece to the other piece. Make sure to pin with the stitching side up because you will need to see the stitches in the next step.

5 Now stitch again, ever so slightly to the left of where you stitched earlier. In this step you are squeezing the piping and this is what is going to make it look nice and clean from the right side.

6 Open up your fabric and check your piping. If you can see some of your stitching, don't worry; just fold your fabric back together and sew a little farther to the left. Check it again and make sure it looks just right!

Make It Just Sew

☺ **Make note of the seam allowance when inserting piping. Most of the seam allowances in this book's patterns are ½" (13mm). Depending on where you decide to add piping, the seam allowance may or may not really matter. But measure your piping seam allowance and make sure that it is the same as the given seam allowance. If not, trim the seam allowance of the piping or move it over to make sure you are allowing for enough seam allowance.**

☺ **When inserting piping between two layers of fabric where one is gathered and one is not, make sure you attach the piping to the non-gathered fabric first.**

☺ **When sewing piping around curves, press the piping in the shape of the curve to make it lay more evenly around the curve. If this doesn't curve the piping enough, clip the piping every ¼" (6mm) or so to help it lay flat around curves and corners. Clip down to the stitching, but make sure not to clip through the stitching.**

GATHERING AND RUFFLES

Knowing how to gather is a very important skill when sewing for little girls. Many of the garments included in this book require gathering. There are several different gathering techniques, but I am going to share the one I have found the most useful when sewing children's clothing.

1. In order to gather fabric for either a ruffle or gathered skirt, you will need to change the stitch length on your sewing machine to the longest length possible. On my machine it is 5.0. Then, increase the tension on your sewing machine to the highest number possible. On my machine that is 9.0.

    If you are gathering a piece of fabric that will be attached to another piece of fabric using a ½"(13mm) seam allowance, sew one row of stitching a ¼"(6mm) away from the edge of the fabric and add a second row of stitching at ½"(13mm). Leave long thread tails at both ends. Do not backstitch at the beginning or end of these rows of stitching, or your threads will not gather.

2. Pull on one or both of the threads to begin gathering. Adjust the gathers by hand until the gathered piece of fabric has reached the desired length.

    If your gathers end up looking more like pleats, your two rows of stitching may be too far apart. Also shorten your stitch length slightly so not as much fabric is pulled up between each stitch. You want your gathers to be done at the exact same seam allowance as your garment so that you will achieve a ruffle and not a pleat.

Make It Just Sew

The ruffler foot is a gathering tool that will make your life much easier. It is definitely not a "must-have" tool, but if you are doing a lot of gathering, this tool may change your life. The foot itself can look a bit intimidating, but it's actually really easy to use. Every sewing machine manufacturer has a ruffler foot that is specifically designed for their machines. The ruffler foot will allow you to gather your fabric and attach it to the fabric at the exact same time. Pretty neat, right?

A ruffler generally has three settings: 12, 6 and 1. What does this mean? Well, it means that the foot will gather the fabric every 12 stitches, every 6 stitches or every 1 stitch. Also, the foot has a knob that can be adjusted that allows you to set the depth of each ruffle. The best way to find out the perfect ruffler settings is to test out several samples made from different fabric weights. Once you have found the settings that work for you, write them down and tape them to the side of your sewing machine for use in the future.

Many overlock machines or sergers also have a similar foot available called a gathering or ruffling foot. The gathering foot gathers the fabric, attaches it to the other non-gathered fabric and serges the edge of both pieces of fabric all at once. This foot has different settings than the ruffler, but again, you can find your ideal settings by running a test strip before sewing your garment. Both of these are great tools to check out.

PINTUCKS

Pintucks add classic charm to any garment. You can make them any size you would like and space them out in many different patterns. While there are specialty sewing feet and twin needles that will make quicker work of corded pintucks, you can also achieve a similar look with your basic sewing machine foot.

Personally, I find it much easier to sew the pintucks on my piece of fabric and then cut out the pattern piece, as opposed to having a pattern piece that requires you to do precise pintucks after the piece is cut out. This way you don't have to worry so much about making sure the tucks are exact, and you have some creative freedom to place the tucks wherever you choose.

Consider cutting out the bib or dress bodice pattern piece from a pintucked piece of fabric. Adding pintucks to your child's garment will garner a timeless, vintage look.

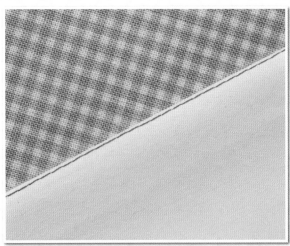

2 Fold the fabric on one of the lines where you would like to make a tuck, wrong sides together. Press the fabric on this line. Edgestitch as close to the folded edge as possible, using approximately a ⅛"–¹⁄₁₆" (3mm–2mm) seam allowance.

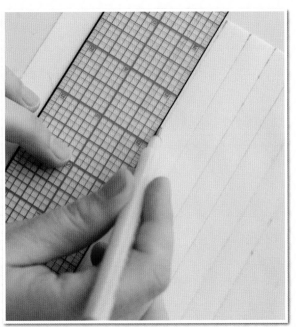

1 Measure out the pattern of lines you would like on your fabric, and mark the lines with a water-soluble fabric marking pen. (Make sure you have enough fabric for the tucks once they are sewn into the fabric.) You can space them however you like. I like to space mine ½" (13mm) apart. Make sure your lines run with the straight of grain (not on the bias).

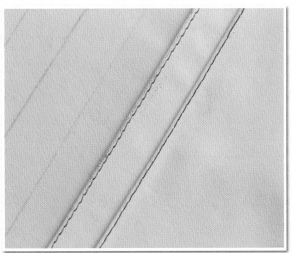

3 Press the tuck to whichever side you would like the tucks to lie. You can arrange them to be pressed in toward the center of the garment or pressed toward the edge of the fabric—it's really up to you.

Once you have made enough tucks in your fabric, cut out the piece and begin garment construction. If you want your pintucks to really stand out, I suggest using a solid fabric, but you can certainly use this technique on a printed fabric as well.

CLIPPING AND NOTCHING CURVES

Garment sewing typically involves sewing many different curves. In order to achieve a professional-looking garment, it is important to make sure all curves are pressed and turned out neatly and smoothly. In order to achieve this, it is important to clip or notch the curves.

If you turn one of your curves right side out and cannot get it to lay flat after pressing it with your iron, you likely haven't clipped or notched out enough. Turn it wrong side out, clip or notch a little bit more, then turn right side out again and see if it lays a little nicer.

When notching and clipping, make sure you use a nice, sharp pair of scissors and cut all the way to the line of stitching, but not through it.

- -

Make It Just Sew

A shortcut I have found that works really well is to trim the seam allowances for curves with a pair of pinking shears. You can cut the seam allowances down to ¼" (6mm) when working with most fabrics. The curve should turn nicely and lay flat without having to do additional clipping or notching.

- -

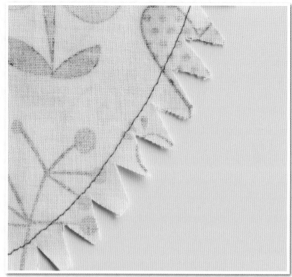

Outer curves: For outer curves, such as Peter Pan collars and curved pockets, you will need to notch out the curve; that is, cut a V shape at several spots in the seam allowance to remove bulk. Removing this bulk will allow the curve to lay smoothly when turned right side out.

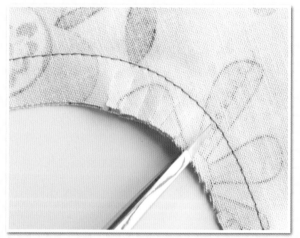

Inner curves: For inner curves, such as necklines and armholes, you will need to clip the curve. To clip a curve, you will not remove any of the seam allowance, but will clip into the fabric so that when the curve is turned right side out, the fabric can spread out and lay flat.

TRIMMING AND TURNING POINTS

Trimming and turning may not seem like a very important technique, but if you are new to sewing garments, I think you will be surprised how often you will use this technique. If your points are not turned out nicely, your garment will not have that precise, professional look you are trying to achieve.

A point-turner is not a must-have, but it's a very nice, inexpensive tool to have on hand. If you don't have one, you can always use a chopstick. Whatever you use, make sure you spend some time turning and trimming your points properly. It will make a difference in the overall finished look of your garment.

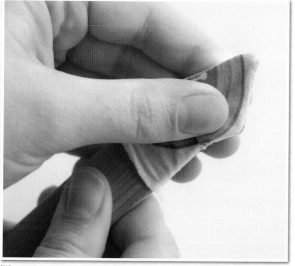

Turning points: Use a point turner or chopstick to get a crisp point when you have turned your piece right side out.

Trimming points: When you have a seam that comes together at a point, such as a waist sash, fabric ties or the corners of a bodice, you need to trim off those points in order to make the point lay flat when turned. Taper down from the sides of the point to remove additional bulk.

Turning tubes: Turning a long tube is easiest with the use of a tube turner. The tube turner has two parts to it: the tube and the stick. To use it, drop the tube down through the opening in the sash and let it fall all the way down to the bottom of the tube. Then, push the stick up through the sewn end through the tube.

BASIC APPLIQUÉ

Appliqué is a unique way to personalize a garment for a little one. You can cut out special shapes, characters or letters and make them part of your child's outfit. You can appliqué the garments you are creating or you can add a simple appliqué to a readymade shirt that might coordinate with another one of the pieces in your child's wardrobe. However you choose to use appliqué, it's a great skill to have in your repertoire.

- -

Make It Just Sew

- ☺ **If you are appliquéing a letter, you need to reverse the letter before tracing it onto the paper-backed fusible web so it will look right once you have appliquéd it to your garment. Also, make sure you notice the direction of the print of the fabric—you want to make sure your appliqué piece doesn't turn out upside down.**

- ☺ **When doing machine embroidery or appliqué, it is important to use a stabilizer to achieve a high-quality, professional look on woven cotton and knit.**

- ☺ **Even if you don't have embroidery capabilities on your sewing machine, you can still use embroidery thread for appliqué. Use a polyester bobbin thread, but change out the top thread for a nicer embroidery thread. This will give your appliqué a beautiful sheen.**

- ☺ **There are many different brands of double-sided fusible interfacing on the market. Some popular brands for this type of appliqué are Steam-A-Seam Lite, Steam-A-Seam Lite 2, and Wonder-Under.**

- -

1 Following the manufacturer's instructions, iron double-sided fusible interfacing to the wrong side of the appliqué fabric. Remove one side of the paper from the interfacing. Place the web-side down on the wrong side of the fabric. Press the fusible web to the fabric using your iron.

2 Trace the shape of the appliqué onto the paper side of the fusible web using a pencil. Cut out the shape and remove the paper.

3 Place the appliqué piece on your garment, right side up. Position and reposition it until it looks just right. Press the top of the appliqué to fuse it to the garment.

4 If you are applying an appliqué to a cotton knit T-shirt or another type of stretchy fabric, make sure you also apply a fusible cutaway or tearaway stabilizer to the wrong side of the garment under the area to be appliquéd (following manufacturer's instructions). The stabilizer will keep the cotton knit from stretching out of shape when you stitch the appliqué.

5 Stitch the appliqué to the garment. There are many options when it comes to finishing the raw edges of your appliqué. I prefer to use a zigzag stitch or a satin stitch (very tight zigzag). Some sewing machines come with an appliqué stitch, or if you prefer a more rustic look, you can do a straight stitch and allow the edges to fray when you wash the garment. Test your stitches before sewing on your appliqué to find one that works for you. Cut away or tear away the stabilizer from the wrong side of the appliqué.

FABRIC YO-YOS

Fabric yo-yos are a great way to add a decorative touch to any garment or accessory. The book includes 3″(8cm) and 5″(13cm) yo-yo circle pattern pieces. The fabric yo-yos can be used to make hair accessories like clips and headbands. You could also consider layering the 3″(8cm) yo-yo on top of the 5″(13cm) one and stitching both to a garment. Add a button to the center of a yo-yo to give it the appearance of a flower.

There are yo-yo-making tools that make very quick work of constructing fabric yo-yos. If you like the look of yo-yos but don't have the time they take to make, definitely check out the many different yo-yo makers on the market.

1 Cut out a circle from the pattern provided.

2 Place the circle with wrong side up. Make sure you use a polyester thread, as cotton thread may tend to break. Knot your thread. Turn in ¼″ (6mm) around the edge of the circle, handsewing close to the edge. Sew a running stitch evenly all the way around the circle.

3 Once you have sewn all the way around the circle, pull the thread lightly to gather into the yo-yo shape.

4 Continue to pull the thread, turning under the inside edges. You might need to work this part a little bit with your hands as you gather.

5 Knot your thread securely to hold the gathers in place. Press your fabric yo-yo. Handstitch yo-yos to a dress or accessory.

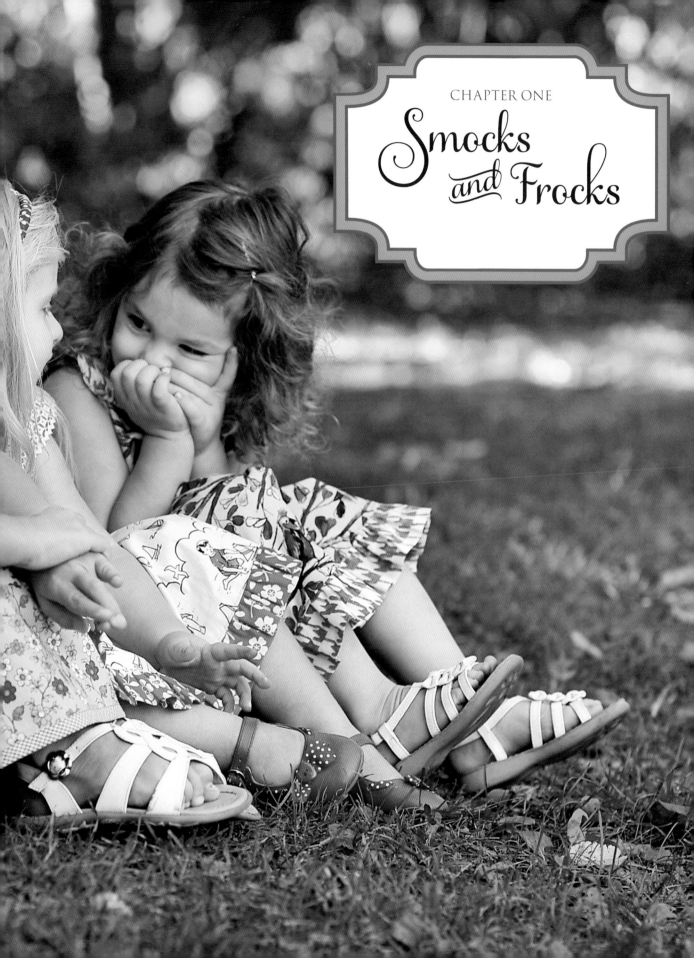

CHAPTER ONE

Smocks and Frocks

Pocket Smock Top

My little girls love pockets—a place to put all their little treasures. Usually those consist of rocks, sticks, little figurines, buttons, coins or anything else they find when we are out and about. Children are the best about treasuring the little things in life that we, as adults, sometimes take for granted.

The Pocket Smock Top was created as an everyday play top for all seasons. The top is longer in length and can be worn sleeveless or layered. Consider pairing it with the Vintage Ruffle Capris or Shorts or the Classic Dress Coat to create different looks in your child's wardrobe.

MATERIALS LIST

- ○ Pocket Smock Top pattern pieces*

- ○ Fabric 1—Yoke Front (#1), Yoke Back (#2), Pocket (#6)

- ○ Fabric 2—Yoke Front Facing (#3), Yoke Back Facing (#4), Lower Front (#5), Lower Back (#5)

- ○ Three 1" (3cm) buttons (back)

- ○ Three ½" (6mm) decorative buttons (front, optional)

- ○ Double-fold bias tape (hem, optional underarm ties)

- ○ Corded piping or trim (optional)

- ○ Coordinating thread

*Specific yardage amounts, layout instructons and pattern pieces found on CD in Pocket Smock Top files.

- -

Make It Just Sew

To finish the bottom edge of the Pocket Smock Top you will need double-fold bias tape. Measure the bottom of the smock to determine how much is needed. Also, if you plan to add in the underarm ties, you will need four additional pieces of double-fold bias tape, each cut 9½" (24cm) long.

- -

1 Fold the pocket pattern piece in half lengthwise with the wrong sides together and press. Mark the pocket stitching lines with a water-soluble marking pen according to the pattern markings.

2 Line up the raw edge of the pocket piece with the right side bottom raw edges of the lower front of the top (Fig. A). Pin to hold in place. Sew down the three pocket lines that you marked previously. Children can be hard on pockets, so make sure to add additional reinforcement stitches at the top of each pocket stitching line. Baste the two sides and bottom edge of the pocket.

3 Run two rows of gathering stitches across the top of the smock skirt pieces (one front and two back pieces).

4 Gather the front skirt so it lines up with the bottom of the front bodice.

5 With right sides together, line up the bottom of the front bodice with the top raw edge of the front skirt piece and sew together (Fig. B). Press the seam up toward the bodice.

6 Topstitch on the bottom edge of the bodice, or if you want to add trim to the front of the smock top, skip the topstitching and sew on the trim at this time.

7 Gather the two back skirt pieces so that they line up with the back bodice pieces. If you plan to add piping or trim into the front or back seam, do so now. (Refer to the Techniques section regarding piping.) Line up the bottom edge of the bodice with the top edge of the skirt, right sides together, and sew in place (Fig. C). Do this for both back pieces. Press seam up toward the bodice. Topstitch toward the bottom edge of both of the bodice backs.

8 Sew the back pieces to the front. Line up the shoulder seams, right sides together, and sew. Do this for the right and left shoulder pieces (Fig. D).

Figure A

Figure B

Figure C

Figure D

Figure E

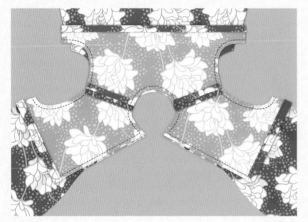

Figure F

Figure G

9 Now construct the bodice facing. With right sides together, line up the shoulder seams of the back facing pieces with the front facing piece and sew together (Fig. E).

10 Hem the bottom of the facing by pressing up a ½" (13mm) and then another ½" (13mm) toward the wrong side of the fabric for the back and front bodice pieces. Sew the hem in place.

11 With right sides together, match the facing and the main bodice. Sew up the back, around the neck and down the other side of the back. Sew the curves of the armholes. Clip corners and curves, turn right side out and press (Fig. F). Topstitch, if desired.

12 Sew the back seam. Line up the back pieces, with the right sides together, and sew from the bottom of the smock up to the bottom of the facing. Press seams open. Sew several reinforcement stitches where the back seams meet the facing to secure (Fig. G).

13 To sew the side seams together, with right sides together, line up the side seams, turning the facing up, and sew from the facing down to the bottom of the lower front (Fig. H). Do this for both sides.

14 Sew buttonholes by machine. Hand sew buttons to the back of the smock according to the pattern markings. If you aren't using fabric-covered shank buttons, you could sew on the buttons by machine as well.

15 To finish the bottom of the smock, apply double-fold bias tape to the bottom edge by unfolding the bias tape and lining up the raw edge of the bias tape with the raw edge of the bottom of the Pocket Smock Top, right sides together (Fig. I). Sew all the way around the bias tape in the seam using a ¼" (6mm) seam allowance—you will be stitching in one of the folds of the bias tape. Stop sewing ½" (13mm) from where you began and overlap the tape by ¼" (6mm). Continue sewing, backstitching at the end. Fold the bias tape over to the wrong side of the fabric, using the previous fold lines as your guide. Edgestitch on top of the bias binding to secure in place. Refer to bias binding application in the Techniques section for more detailed instruction.

16 Embellish the front bodice with buttons, if you so choose, or use any other embellishment that will make your piece truly unique.

Figure H

Figure I

Make It Just Sew: Taking the Pocket Smock Top a Step Further

At this point your Pocket Smock Top is complete. But, if you'd like to take the garment a step further, simply complete the following steps to add a gathered casing with a bow under each arm. Doing so will create a more fitted top.

1. Pull the facing and the main dress apart under both arms. Make two ½"(13mm) buttonholes on either side of each side seam on the exterior fabric. The buttonholes should be ½"(13mm) apart from each other and ½"(13mm) down from the underarm seam as well. The buttonholes are made in the dress part only. Make sure the facing is moved well out of the way. Once you've made your buttonholes (there should be a total of four, two under each armhole), cut the buttonholes open.

2. Make the fabric ties. Cut four pieces of double-fold bias tape, 9½"(24cm) long. Open up the bias tape and fold in one short end of each piece ¼"(6mm) toward the wrong side. Then fold in the folded edge to form a point. Refold the tape in half and edgestitch the double-fold bias tape closed. You could also substitute the bias tape for ribbon. Just make sure to use some kind of sealer on the ends to prevent fraying.

3. With the facing and bodice wrong sides together, stitch a casing ½"(13mm) from the side seam and ¾"(19mm) from the armhole edge all the way around the armhole. Stop sewing ½"(13mm) before the side seam.

4. Using a bodkin or safety pin, with the raw edge going in first, thread each one of the ties through one of the buttonholes. Once the tie is threaded and the raw end extends ¼"(6mm) past the end of the casing, stitch the end of the casing closed. This will catch the raw end of the fabric tie, yet the finished end will still be poking out of the buttonhole (Fig. J). Do this for all four ties.

5. Once all four ties are secured in place, tie them in a bow under each arm.

Figure J

Play Frock

Ring Around the Rosy is one of my little ladies' favorite songs to sing with their girlfriends. The way they giggle when they "all fall down" is something that will stay in my mind forever. Those precious moments of early girlhood bring back such a nostalgic, warm feeling. Oh, if we could only keep them young forever!

While little girls love to wear pretty dresses, they also like to be comfy. The Play Frock is an easy to wear dress that is perfect for a casual day at home, school, the playground, or it can even be dressed up for special occasions. This versatile dress is perfect for all seasons as it can be layered for colder weather and worn as a sleeveless dress for warmer months. The skirt portion of the frock is left plain, but you can easily add a pocket or appliqué design, if you like.

MATERIALS LIST

- ○ Pocket Smock Top pattern pieces* (cut at frock length; eliminate pocket pieces)

- ○ Fabric 1—Yoke Front (#1), Yoke Back (#2)

- ○ Fabric 2—Yoke Front Facing (#3), Yoke Back Facing (#4), Lower Front (#5), Lower Back (#5)

- ○ Three 1" (3cm) buttons (back)

- ○ Double-fold bias tape (optional underarm ties)

- ○ Corded piping or trim (optional)

- ○ Coordinating thread

*Specific yardage amounts, layout instructons and pattern pieces found on CD in Pocket Smock Top files.

- -

Make It Just Sew

Because it doesn't have the extra bulk of a pocket layer, the Play Frock design can be constructed from a variety of different fabrics. Consider using quilting weight cotton, chambray, linen, madras or seersucker for warmer months, and corduroy, tweed, wool or velveteen for cooler weather.

- -

1 Cut out the frock using the same pattern pieces as the Pocket Smock Top, but use the frock-length cutting line. The frock is constructed in the same manner as the Pocket Smock Top, but omit any steps involving the pockets. As with the Pocket Smock Top, the underarm casing is completely optional depending on the look you are hoping to achieve.

2 You can choose to finish the hem with bias tape (as in the previous look) or you can do a more traditional hem. For a traditional hem, fold the bottom edge up ½" (13mm) toward the wrong side of the fabric, then up another ½" (13mm) and sew in place.

  A third option to finish the hem is with a contrast band of fabric. To add the contrast band, reduce the cutting length of the main dress by 2½" (6cm) and cut two pieces of contrasting fabric 4"(10cm) wide by the width of the dress. Place the contrast band fabric pieces with the right sides together and sew at the two short, raw ends. Press the seams open and press the contrast band in half lengthwise with wrong sides together so that the two raw edges line up. Line up the raw edge of the bottom of the dress and the raw edge of the contrast band so that the fold in the contrast band is pointing up toward the main dress. Sew the contrast band to dress using a ½" (13mm) seam allowance. Finish the edge with a zigzag stitch or a serger. Press the seam up toward the dress and press the contrast band down. Topstitch on the bottom of the main part of the dress or sew a fun piece of trim on top of the seam. The contrast band eliminates the need for a traditional hem. You can choose to do a wider or more narrow contrast band—just adjust your dress length accordingly. You could also apply the contrast band in the same way you apply the bias binding/tape, which would encase all the raw edges of the dress and the contrast band.

3 If you'd like, add decorative ribbon or trim ½" (13mm) up from the bottom hem. Choose something unique and different for your special little lady.

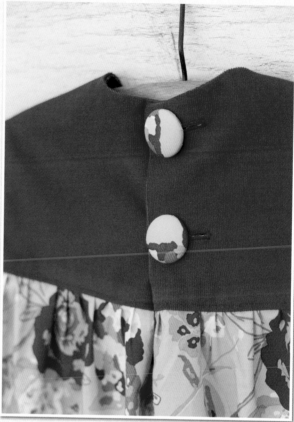

Make It Just Sew

Consider using fabric as part of your trim. The center of the bodice on the Play Frock shown here has a strip of fabric trimmed out with two pieces of rickrack and a piece of woven trim sewn down the center of the fabric strip. The trim embellishment is added to the bodice front prior to garment construction. Layering trims in this manner is a way to create custom trim that will truly be one of a kind.

Dress pictured with Double Ruffle Capris (Chapter 2).

Swing Smock

THE SWING SMOCK IS A more simplistic version of the Pocket Smock Top. This design eliminates the pocket and gives you the option of adding different unique trims at the bottom hem. This top can also be made with or without the gathered underarm ties; of course, there is more "swing" to the top without the ties! It's a versatile piece that pairs well with many other pieces in the book and even looks great with a pair of jeans.

AGAIN, YOU CAN CHOOSE TO finish the hem with bias tape or a traditional hem as done with the Frock, but I suggest that you consider adding some trim at the bottom hem of the top to add further interest to the garment. Some trim options include rickrack, cotton loopy trim, pom-poms, crochet edging, lace, pre-gathered eyelet or ruffles.

MATERIALS LIST

- ○ Pocket Smock Top pattern pieces* (eliminate pocket piece)
- ○ Fabric 1—Yoke Front (#1), Yoke Back (#2)
- ○ Fabric 2—Yoke Front Facing (#3), Yoke Back Facing (#4), Lower Front (#5), Lower Back (#5)
- ○ Three 1" (3cm) buttons (back)
- ○ Double-fold bias tape (optional, if not adding trim at hem)
- ○ Piping or trim (optional, if not using double-fold bias tape at hem)
- ○ Coordinating thread

*Specific yardage amounts, layout instructons and pattern pieces found on CD in Pocket Smock Top files.

1 Cut out the necessary pattern pieces and construct the Swing Smock in the same manner as the Pocket Smock Top, but eliminate the steps involving the front pocket.

2 Add bias binding or decorative trim to the bottom hem. If adding trim, press the bottom hem up ½" (13mm) toward the wrong side of the fabric. Line up the trim with the bottom hem on the right side of the fabric (if using something such as rickrack). Stitch down the center of the trim all the way around the bottom of the top, making sure to tuck in the raw edges when joining the two ends.

3 Press the trim and dress hem open, pressing the trim toward the wrong side of the frock. This will cause whatever trim you are using to just peek through at the hem. Edgestitch or topstitch around the bottom of the dress in coordinating thread to secure the trim in place.

- -

Make It Just Sew

When constructing the Swing Smock, pay careful attention to the width of your trim. While this top was designed with a very forgiving hem, you may not be able to line it up with the edge of the top if you're using a larger trim. Always keep this in mind when selecting your trim. See the Techniques section for more detailed information about working with trims.

- -

Dress pictured with Fabric-Covered Button Headband (Chapter 6).

Round Neck Ruffle Dress

LITTLE GIRLS LOVE TO TWIRL. Isn't that what makes us love dresses when we are little? The Round Neck Ruffle Dress has a big twirl factor and is sure to become one of your girls' very favorite dresses.

THIS DRESS OFFERS A LOT of fun ways to play with patterned fabrics and trims. For a more eclectic look, try using a number of different prints. Or, for a more subtle look, try using just two prints—one for the main dress and another for the collar.

THIS DRESS CAN BE TRIMMED and embellished very easily. You can add woven ribbon trim around any of the bottom tiers. Also, the bodice is large enough to accommodate an embroidered monogram for that personalized touch. The trim on the collar is completely optional, but is a fun little detail. You can use piping, rickrack, picot edging and so much more.

MATERIALS LIST

- ○ Ruffle Dress/Skirt pattern pieces* (eliminate sash)
- ○ Fabric 1—Collar (#1)
- ○ Fabric 2—Front Bodice (#2), Bodice Back (#3)
- ○ Fabric 3—Top Tier (#4)
- ○ Fabric 4—Middle Tier (#5)
- ○ Fabric 5—Bottom Tier (#6)
- ○ Single-fold bias tape (several inches longer than the inside of the collar)
- ○ Three 1" (3cm) buttons (back)
- ○ Corded piping or decorative trim (collar, optional)
- ○ Coordinating thread

*Specific yardage amounts, layout instructons and pattern pieces found on CD in Ruffle Dress and Skirt files.

Make It Just Sew

You will need single-fold bias tape to finish the raw edge of the collar. You can make your own to match the dress exactly by following the bias tape instructions in the Techniques section of the book, or you can purchase store-bought bias tape in a coordinating color.

1 To make the top tier, place both pieces right sides together and sew them together along both short sides (Fig. A). Do the same for the middle tier. For the bottom tier, sew together all four pieces by sewing them each together along the short side, again with right sides together. For all three tiers you will have a separate circular, skirtlike piece of fabric.

2 Run two rows of gathering stitches around the top of the middle tier. Gather the fabric until it is the same width as the bottom edge of the top tier. Refer to the Techniques section for gathering tips.

3 Place the top tier inside the middle tier, right sides together. Line up the top edge of the middle tier and the bottom edge of the top tier. Adjust the gathers so they are spaced evenly, lining up the side seams (Fig. B). Sew the top tier to the middle tier and press the seam up toward the top tier. Topstitch around the bottom of the top tier through all layers.

4 With wrong sides together, fold the bottom tier in half lengthwise. Run two rows of gathering stitches along the top, raw edge of the bottom tier through both layers.

5 Gather the bottom tier until it is the same width as the bottom of the middle tier. Line up the raw edge of the bottom tier with the bottom raw edge of the middle tier, right sides together, and pin in place (Fig. C). Stitch all the way around, making sure that all the gathers are evenly spaced. Press the seam up toward the middle tier.

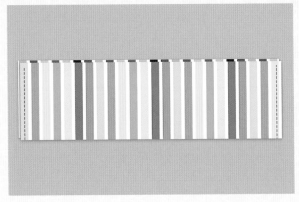

Figure A

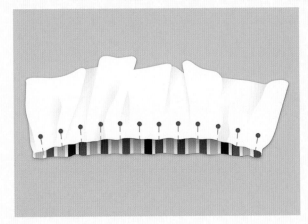

Figure B

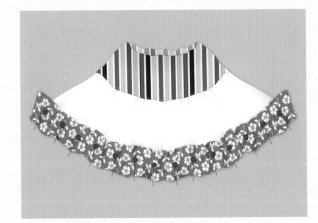

Figure C

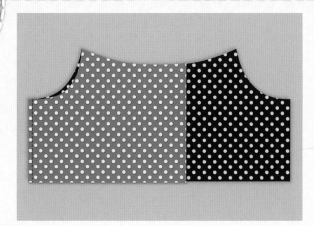

Figure D

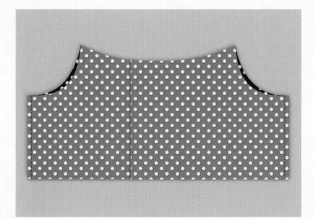

Figure E

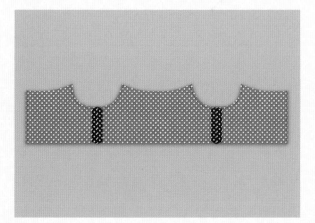

Figure F

6 Topstitch along the bottom of the middle tier, right above the bottom tier.

7 Run two rows of gathering stitches along the top of the top tier (this will be needed in a later step).

8 Now construct the bodice. Place one back piece on top of the front bodice, right sides together, and sew at the side seam (Fig. D). Repeat to sew the other side (Fig. E). Repeat to make the bodice lining.

9 Place the bodice lining and the bodice piece right sides together, and sew along the two straight side seams and under both underarm seams (Fig. F). Clip the underarm curves, turn right side out and press. Edgestitch or topstitch the curve under each armhole.

10 Next, construct the round collar piece. If you would like to add any trim into the seam, you will need to do that first. Baste the trim to the right side of one of the round collar pieces, making sure to adjust the trim for the seam allowance (see the Trims and Embellishments section for more information) (Fig. G).

11 Place the two round collar pieces right sides together and sew along the two short sides (Fig. H).

12 Attach the round collar to the bodice. Place the top of the bodice in between the two round collar pieces. Line up the raw edges of the top of the bodice and the outer curve of the round collar (the side where you basted your trim). If you are using trim in the collar, make sure to place the trim side right sides together with the front of the bodice. Pin in place and sew all the way around the outer curve, leaving the inner curve unfinished. Clip curves, turn collar right side out and press (Fig. I).

- -

Make It Just Sew

To make your life easier, mark the center of the collar and the center of the bodice with your fabric marking pen. Pin the collar sides to the bodice sides and pin the center collar and center bodice, and continue pinning from there out.

- -

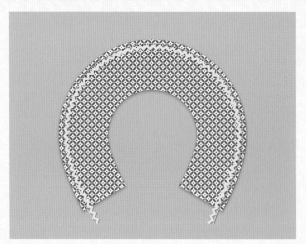

Figure G

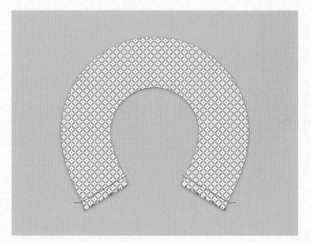

Figure H

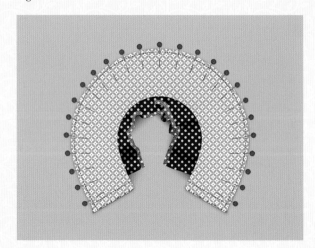

Figure I

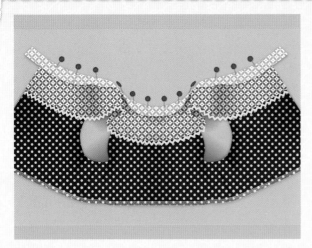

Figure J

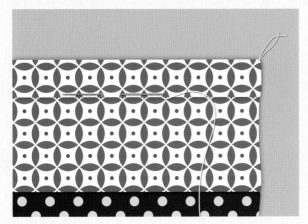

Figure K

13 Finish the raw neck edge of the collar using a strip of single-fold bias tape that measures a bit longer than the length of the inner curve of the collar. Unfold the bias tape and, with right sides together, line up the raw edge of the top of the collar with a raw edge of the bias tape (Fig. J). Sew the bias tape to collar using a ¼" (6mm) seam allowance (stitch in the fold of the bias tape). Refer to the Techniques section for additional information on applying bias tape.

14 Fold bias tape over to the lining side of the collar encasing the raw edge. Fold in the raw ends of the bias tape and slipstitch the bias tape to the back of the collar (Fig. K). Using a slipstitch will keep you from seeing any stitching on the front of the collar.

15 Mark buttonhole placement on the back of the dress and collar, and sew buttonholes according to pattern markings. Stitch buttons onto the opposite side of the dress. Once you've sewn on the buttons, button the back of the bodice and add a basting stitch along the bottom edge where the back bodice pieces overlap.

16 To sew the bodice and skirt together, gather the top tier so it is the same width as the bodice. Turn the skirt inside out and place the bodice inside the skirt. The top of the bodice (the collar) will be pointing down toward the bottom of the skirt. With right sides together, line up the raw edge of the bodice with the raw edge of the top tier of the skirt. Sew the pieces together. Then turn the dress right side out and press the seam up toward the bodice. Add topstitching along the bottom edge of the bodice.

Make It Just Sew

Buttons offer a great way to get creative with your dress design. Using fabric-covered buttons can add a lot of vintage charm, but novelty buttons can lend a bit of whimsy. Don't overlook the buttons—they are the finishing touches on your garment.

Twirl Skirt

IF YOUR LITTLE LADY LIKES dresses, I'm going to guess that she likes skirts, too. My two girls absolutely adore this tiered ruffle twirl skirt! The Twirl Skirt is constructed just as the Round Neck Ruffle Dress, yet instead of attaching the three tiers to the bodice, you will be sewing a casing in the top tier and threading elastic through the top. You can also add an optional fabric sash that can be tied in the front or back.

THIS SKIRT HAS MAJOR TWIRL factor just like the Round Neck Ruffle Dress, so if your little girl is a twirler, she will want this skirt! Consider using multiple printed fabrics or choose one single favorite print. Some suggested fabrics are quilting-weight cotton, linen or corduroy. Pair this skirt with an embellished T-shirt and headband for a complete look.

MATERIALS LIST

- ○ Ruffle Dress/Skirt pattern pieces* (three tier pieces, sash optional)
- ○ Fabric 1—Top Tier (#4)
- ○ Fabric 2—Middle Tier (#5)
- ○ Fabric 3—Bottom Tier (#6), Sash (#7)
- ○ ½" (13mm) elastic (waistband; see sidebar)
- ○ Bodkin or safety pin
- ○ Coordinating thread

*Specific yardage amounts, layout instructons and pattern pieces found on CD in Ruffle Dress and Skirt files.

Make It Just Sew: Elastic Sizing

Use the following measurements as a guide for cutting your elastic.

Size 12 Months: 18" (46cm)

Size 2T: 19" (48cm)

Size 4T: 20" (51cm)

Size 6: 21" (53cm)

Size 8: 22" (56cm)

Size 10: 23" (58cm)

Remember, these are approximate measurements. Every child is a little different. The finished elastic measurement will be 1" (3cm) shorter than the cutting measurement. If you have the child you are sewing for nearby, it would be a good idea to measure her waist prior to cutting the elastic to make sure that length will work for them.

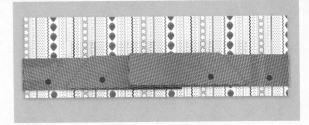

1 Cut two sash pieces. Fold one sash piece in half lengthwise with right sides together and sew down the long edge to the point, leaving the shorter edge open for turning. Repeat for the other piece.

Figure A

2 Turn the sash right side out. (The easiest way to turn sashes is with a tube turner. Refer to the Tools of the Trade section.) Press the sash, and edgestitch or topstitch the sash.

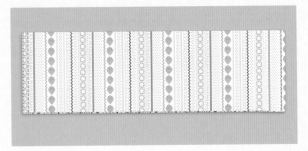

3 Measure down 2½" (6cm) along the short ends on one piece of the top tier, right side up, and mark. Place one sash piece at the 2½" (6cm) mark and match the raw edges. Repeat on the other side of the top tier piece (Fig. A).

Figure B

4 With right sides together, place the other top tier piece on top of the piece with the basted sash pieces and sew the two short side seams (Fig. B).

5 Follow steps 1–3 of the Round Neck Ruffle Dress instructions to construct and assemble the rest of the tiers.

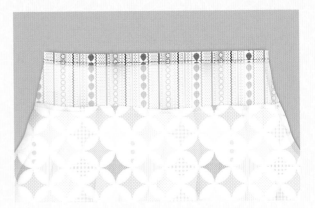

6 For the bottom tier, instead of folding it in half, sew a traditional hem. Fold the bottom raw edge up ½" (13mm) toward the wrong side of the fabric and then up another ½" (13mm). Sew in place. If you have a serger, a rolled hem would work nicely for the bottom tier; just make sure to adjust the length of the skirt accordingly.

Figure C

7 Once you have sewn all three tiers together, fold down the top tier ¼" (6mm) toward the wrong side of the skirt; then fold it down again by ¾" (19mm) to make the casing for the elastic. Sew all the way around using ¾" (19mm) seam allowance, leaving a 2" (5cm) opening (Fig. C).

8 Cut ½" (13mm) wide elastic for the waistband in the desired size (see sidebar on previous page).

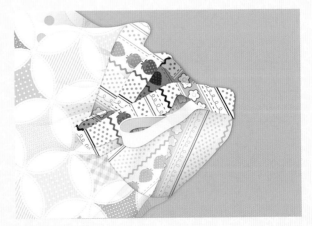

9 Using a bodkin or safety pin, thread the elastic through the casing (Fig. D). Overlap the two ends by 1" (3cm) and sew together using several rows of zigzag stitches. Sew the opening in the casing closed.

10 Tie the fabric sash in a bow in the front or back of the skirt and let your little lady twirl to her heart's content!

Figure D

Skirt pictured with Embellished Bib Shirt and Vintage Style Hair Accessory (Chapter 6).

CHAPTER TWO

You Bet Your Britches

Capris pictured with Classic A-Line Dress/Top (Chapter 4).

Vintage Ruffle Capris and Shorts

As much as little girls love dresses, there are times when only pants or shorts will do. These darling Vintage Ruffle Capris and Shorts are perfect for so many occasions. You can choose to make the pattern as a capri or shorts, perfect for the warmer weather months. Or, make them in a heavy-weight fabric as a banded knicker or bloomer short to layer with tights and boots during cooler weather. Either way, the unique pockets and small ruffles are fun, feminine details.

Your choice of fabric is what's going to create a truly unique, one-of-a-kind look. Feel free to pair different patterned fabrics together, but be sure to consider fabric scale when selecting printed fabrics. Choose one main print for the larger pattern pieces and a smaller-scale print for the accents. Solid fabrics are also a great option. Some suggested fabrics would be quilting-weight cotton, seersucker, lightweight denim, velvet or velveteen (for a dressier look), tweed, soft wool, linen, madras or cotton twill.

Try pairing these bottoms with the Pocket Smock Top, Swing Smock, Classic Dress Coat, Classic A-Line Top or any embellished shirt to create different looks in your child's wardrobe. Or keep it simple and pair with a favorite solid colored T-shirt, tank top or blouse.

Make It Just Sew

The Vintage Ruffle Capris and Shorts are a wonderful base pattern for you to get creative. Consider adding some trim such as rickrack or piping in between the ruffle and the main part of the capris or shorts. You can also use the same trim in between the waistband and the main part of the pants as well. Also, you can opt to eliminate the pocket on the back side, but instead you can add it to the side of the Capri for a girly cargo pant look. You could even lengthen the Capris to a full-length pant by using an existing pair of pants that fits your child as your length cutting guide. Whatever you do, have fun with this pattern and make it your own!

Make It Just Sew: Elastic Sizing

Use the following measurements as a guide for cutting your elastic.

Size 12 Months: 7½" (19cm)

Size 2T: 8" (20cm)

Size 4T: 8½" (22cm)

Size 6: 9" (23cm)

Size 8: 9½" (24cm)

Size 10: 10" (25cm)

Remember, these are approximate measurements. Every child is a little different. The finished elastic measurement will be 1" (3cm) shorter than the cutting measurement. If you have the child you are sewing for nearby, it would be a good idea to measure her waist prior to cutting the elastic to make sure that length will work for them.

MATERIALS LIST

- ❍ Ruffle Capris/Shorts pattern pieces*
- ❍ Fabric 1—Front (#1), Back (#2), Back Pocket (#3)
- ❍ Fabric 2—Front Pocket (#4), Front Pocket Facing (#5), Back Pocket Ruffle (#6), Front Waistband (#7), Back Waistband (#8), Bottom Ruffle (#10)
- ❍ Four ½"–1" (13mm–3cm) buttons
- ❍ Bodkin or safety pin
- ❍ ½" or ¾" (13mm or 19mm) elastic
- ❍ Coordinating thread

*Specific yardage amounts, layout instructons and pattern pieces found on CD in Ruffle Capris and Shorts files. These are slightly fitted capris and shorts through the hip. Please select your child's size based on their waist measurement and adjust the length accordingly.

1 To construct the pockets, place the pocket facing together with the front of the pant, right sides together. Sew along the curve. Clip the curves. Make sure to cut almost all the way down to the stitching where the curve dips in the pocket. If you do not cut close enough, it will not turn out properly (Fig. A).

2 Turn the front of the pant and the facing right side out. Press out the curves. Edgestitch along the curve. Repeat the first two steps for the other side of the pants.

3 The buttons on the front pockets can be faux buttons or functional buttons. For functional buttons, make your buttonholes on the front of the pants according to pattern markings. Then, sew the buttons onto the actual pocket according to button placement markings on the pattern. If you prefer faux buttons, wait to sew on the buttons until after step 4.

4 With right sides together, place the main pocket piece on top of the pocket-facing piece. Separate the facing from the main pants piece and sew around the curve (Fig. B). Make sure to move the main part of the pants out of the way so you don't stitch on the front of the pants. However, if you like that look, you could certainly add the stitching to the front of the pants.

5 If you have not added your buttons yet, do so at this time. Sew the buttons on the front of the pants according to pattern markings, making sure to sew through the back pocket part as well. This will make a faux-button pocket.

6 To construct the back pocket, place the two ruffle pieces right sides together, and sew along the long curved side using a ¼" (6mm) seam allowance, leaving the straight side open. Clip the curves, turn right side out and press.

7 Run two rows of gathering stitches through both layers along the top, raw edge of the ruffle. Gather the ruffle so that it is about 1" (3cm) smaller than the curve of the pocket (Fig. C).

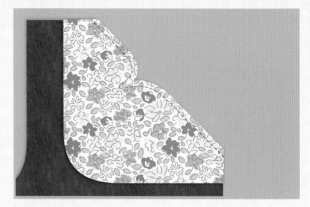

Figure A

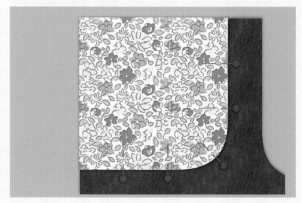

Figure B

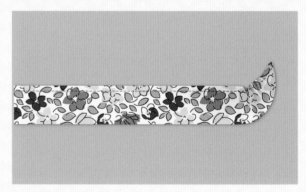

Figure C

Figure D

Figure E

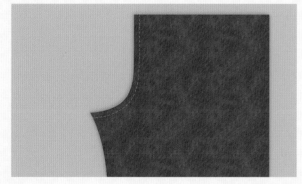

Figure F

8 Beginning ½" (13mm) from the top edge, pin the ruffle to one back pocket piece along the curve, lining up the raw edges, and end ½" (13mm) from the top of the curve on the other side. (This ensures that you won't catch the curve of the ruffle in the seam when sewing the two pocket pieces together.) Baste the ruffle in place (Fig. D).

9 Place the remaining pocket piece on top with right sides together, sandwiching the ruffle in between both pocket pieces (Fig. E). Sew all the way around the pocket, leaving a 1"–2" (3cm–5cm) opening along the curve of the pocket. Clip the curves, and cut almost down to the stitching on the dip in the back pocket, just as you did for the front pockets, to make sure it turns out smoothly. Turn right side out and press. Press under the 1"–2" (3cm–5cm) that you left open so that it lines up nicely with the rest of the pocket.

10 If you'd like, edgestitch along the top of the pocket before you sew the pocket to the pants. This is completely optional.

Pin the pocket in place according to pattern placement and edgestitch all the way around the sides and bottom. Sew reinforcement stitches at the top corners of the pocket.

11 To construct the pants, place the front pant pieces right sides together and sew the center front seam (Fig. F). Repeat with the back pants pieces. Open up the front and the back of the pants. Place the front of the pants and the back of the pants right sides together and sew the inner leg—up one side and down the other. Finally, sew the pants together at the side seams (Fig. G). Turn right side out and press.

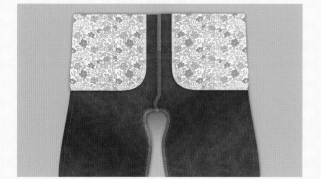

Figure G

12 To add the waistband, place the waistband pieces right sides together and sew both short edges together (Fig. H). The shorter piece will be the front waistband, and the longer piece will be the back waistband. Once you have sewn the front and back together, press the waistband in half lengthwise with the wrong sides together.

13 Next, open the waistband back up and insert elastic in the back of the waistband. Pin the elastic to each of the side seams, allowing it to extend past the back waistband piece by ½" (13mm) on each side. With the waistband still open, stitch on top of the side seams. Make sure you sew several lines of stitches on top of each other so that the elastic is completely secure. Fold the waistband piece back in half.

14 Line up the raw edges of the waistband with the top raw edge of the pants (Fig I). You will need to stretch the elastic in the back waistband while you sew. Sew all the way around and press the waistband up. The elastic will now be encased in the back of the waistband. You can use a zigzag stitch or a serger to finish the raw edges if you would like.

You could also apply the waistband as you would bias tape by sewing the outer waistband to the pants, folding over the interior waistband to the inside. Fold under a ½" (13mm) of the inner waistband toward the wrong side of the fabric. Then run a row of topstitching ¼" (6mm) from the bottom of the waistband. This will encase all raw edges of the pants top and waistband. Just don't catch the elastic in your stitching!

15 Place the bottom ruffle pieces right sides together and sew along the curved side using a ¼" (6mm) seam allowance. Clip the curve and turn the piece right side out. Run two rows of gathering stitches along the raw edge, and gather until the ruffle is about 1" (3cm) longer than the circumference of the bottom leg of the pants.

16 Starting at the pants side seam, with right sides together, pin the raw edge of the ruffle to the bottom raw edge of the pants. Overlap the curved ends of the ruffle by ½" (13mm) at the outer side seam (Fig. J). Sew the ruffle to the pants. Press the ruffle down and the seam up toward the pants, and edgestitch or topstitch around the bottom of the pant leg.

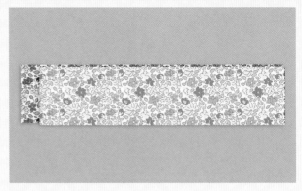
Figure H

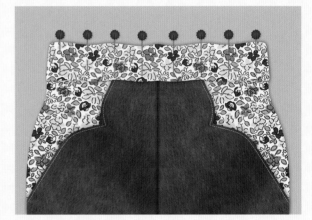
Figure I

Figure J

Capris pictured with Classic A-Line Dress/Top (Chapter 4).

Make It Just Sew: Ruffle Shorts Variation

For the Shorts variation, construct the Shorts in the exact same way as the Capris, but cut the pattern along the shorter cutting line prior to construction. The Shorts are meant to fall right above the knee. If you would prefer a shorter length, you will need to shorten the pattern cutting line prior to construction.

Banded Bloomer Shorts
and Knickers

BLOOMERS AND KNICKERS ARE SO timeless and sweet. Just like the other pieces in this book, they work well for all seasons. I always love to put some kind of shorts or bloomers under my girls' dresses. As much as we tell our little ladies to keep their dresses down, sometimes those monkey bars are hard to resist. Consider making several pairs to mix and match with different outfits.

IF YOU WOULD LIKE TO make these as bottoms to be worn on their own, there's an extra sash pattern piece to use with the Capris, Shorts, or Knickers. This sash is inserted at the side seams and can be tied in the front or the back depending on your preference. If you want to add a little whimsy to your little lady's outfit, add the sash—she'll love it!

IF YOU WOULD PREFER TO make these shorts as a banded bloomer, you may want to reduce the length of the shorts by 1"–2" (3cm–5cm) depending on the size you are making and the length you would like your bloomers. If you want a fuller bloomer or knicker, I suggest sizing up one size in the width, but keeping their true size in the length. Also, plan to use your elastic measurement for your child's true size as well. You can choose to keep the pockets as with the Vintage Ruffle Capris, but you can also make them without the pockets. The possibilities are endless!

MATERIALS LIST

○ Ruffle Capris/Shorts pattern pieces* (eliminate Bottom Ruffle [#10])

○ Optional: Pockets (#3–#6) and Tab (#9)

○ Fabric 1—Front (#1), Back (#2), Back Pocket (#3)

○ Fabric 2—Front Pocket (#4), Front Pocket Facing (#5), Back Pocket Ruffle (#6), Front Waistband (#7), Back Waistband (#8)

○ Two sash pieces (optional; pattern from Ruffle Dress/Skirt pattern set, piece #7, cut from Fabric 2)

○ Four ½"–1"(13mm–3cm) buttons

○ Bodkin or safety pin

○ ½" or ¾" (13mm–19mm) elastic (see Elastic Sizing chart for Vintage Ruffle Capris and Shorts project)

○ Double-fold bias tape (two pieces cut 1"–2" [3cm–5cm] smaller than the circumference of the leg opening)

○ Coordinating thread

Specific yardage amounts, layout instructons and pattern pieces found on CD in Ruffle Capris and Shorts files.

Make It Just Sew

The Banded Bloomer Shorts and Knickers are constructed exactly the same way, except you will use the shorts cutting line for the Bloomers and the Capri cutting line for the Knickers.

In order to adapt the pattern to a pant or short with no pockets, you will need to alter the pattern slightly. Instead of cutting along the curved line for the pocket, cut straight up the side, matching up with the center-top of the capris. Do not cut any of the pocket pattern pieces, unless of course, you would like to add one to the back of the pants or shorts.

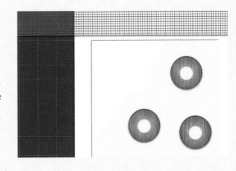

1 Cut two sash pieces. Fold one sash piece in half lengthwise with right sides together and sew down the long edge to the point, leaving the shorter edge open for turning. Repeat for the other piece (Fig. A).

2 Turn the sash right side out using a tube turner. Press the sash once it is turned right side out and edgestitch or topstitch the sash.

3 Sew the front of the shorts together at the center curved seam. Do the same for the back of the shorts (Fig. B). Then, sew the front and the back of the shorts together at the crotch seam (Fig. C).

4 Pin the two sashes to the front of the shorts on both sides. Line up the raw edge of the sash with the raw edge of the side seam of the bloomer shorts, measuring down 1"(3cm) from the top of the shorts (Fig. D). The finished side of the sashes will be pointing inward. Baste the sashes in place.

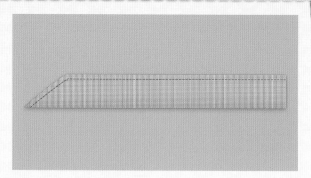

Figure A

Figure B

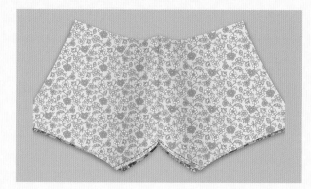

Figure C

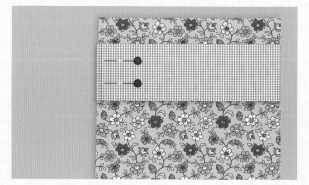

Figure D

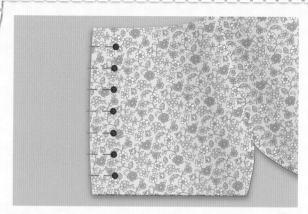

Figure E

Figure F

5 Place the bloomer shorts with right sides together and sew down both side seams. The sash pieces will be caught in these side seams (Fig. E).

6 Cut two pieces of double-fold bias tape 1"–2" (3cm–5cm) smaller than the leg openings. (Make sure to measure your child's leg right below the knee for the knickers and mid-thigh for the bloomer shorts to make sure the bias tape measurement is not too small for them.) To gather the legs of the bloomer shorts, run two rows of gathering stitches around the bottom of each leg opening. Open out the double-fold bias tape and turn in ¼" (6mm) at one end. Beginning with the folded edge, pin the tape to the gathered edge of the shorts, matching raw edges. Overlap the ends of the tape at the end (Fig. F). Sew in the fold, ¼" (6mm) away from the raw edges.

7 Fold the bias tape over to the wrong side of the fabric and pin it in place. Again, make sure the fold at the beginning of the bias tape encases the raw edge of the end of the bias tape. Edgestitch around the bias tape of both leg openings.

8 Apply the waistband as described in steps 12–14 for the Vintage Ruffle Capris and Shorts.

Make It Just Sew

If you would prefer a more gathered look for the Bloomer Shorts and Knickers, reduce the length of the bias binding. This may not work for all children, depending on the size of their legs. Just make sure to measure your child's leg, either at the thigh for the Shorts or below the knee for the Knickers, and then adjust your bias binding measurement accordingly.

Shorts pictured with navy blue Embellished Bib Shirt
(Chapter 6) and Play Frock (Chapter 1).

Banded Shorts *and* Capris

THE BANDED SHORTS AND CAPRIS are constructed just as the Vintage Ruffle Capris and Shorts, but cut at the shorts or capri length. Another important difference between the two is the hem. For this variation, the hem is finished with double-fold bias tape with no gathering.

THESE SHORTS WORK GREAT FOR all ages. They are also a wonderful option if your little lady isn't wild about ruffles, as they are more subtle than the Vintage Ruffle pieces.

MATERIALS LIST

- ❍ Ruffle Capris and Shorts pattern pieces* (eliminate Bottom Ruffle [#10])

- ❍ Optional: Pockets (#3–#6) and Tab (#9)

- ❍ Fabric 1—Front (#1), Back (#2), Back Pocket (#3)

- ❍ Fabric 2—Front Pocket (#4), Front Pocket Facing (#5), Back Pocket Ruffle (#6), Front Waistband (#7), Back Waistband (#8)

- ❍ Two sash pieces (optional; pattern from Ruffle Dress/Skirt pattern set, piece #7, cut from Fabric 2)

- ❍ Four ½"–1" (13mm–3cm) buttons

- ❍ Bodkin or safety pin

- ❍ ½" or ¾" (13mm–19mm) elastic (see Elastic Sizing chart for Vintage Ruffle Capris and Shorts project)

- ❍ Trim for leg binding (optional)

- ❍ Double-fold bias tape (two pieces cut 1" (3cm) larger than the circumference of the leg opening)

- ❍ Coordinating thread

*Specific yardage amounts, layout instructons and pattern pieces found on CD in Ruffle Capris and Shorts files.

1 Construct the Shorts as described for the Vintage Ruffle Shorts or add in the sash as with the Banded Bloomer Shorts and Knickers, but eliminate the ruffle. Instead, cut two pieces of double-fold bias tape 1" (3cm) longer than the leg circumference. Apply bias tape according to the Techniques section, referring to the Banded Bloomer Shorts and Capris for how to join the two raw ends.

2 Add any embellishments, like side button tabs, right above the bias tape (found in the following project instructions for the Double Ruffle Capris).

- -

Make It Just Sew

For the Banded Shorts and Capris you have the option of using all one fabric or using one fabric for the main shorts/capris and a contrasting fabric for the leg band and waistband. If you are using all one fabric, consider breaking up the leg band and the main shorts/capris by adding rickrack or piping into the seam between the two (as pictured here with the shorts accompanying the Little Lady Coat). It's a fun, whimsical little detail.

- -

Pants pictured with Pocket Smock Top (Chapter 1).

Double Ruffle Capris

The Double Ruffle Capris are easily modified for an entirely different look for your little one. Let's just say these definitely add a little more flair! Again, the same options apply as in some of the previous designs. You can make these bottoms without the pockets, add a different ruffle, include the side button tabs or add the optional fabric sash with a whimsical bow. You can also use pre-gathered lace, eyelet or other trim as one of your ruffle layers.

MATERIALS LIST

- Ruffle Capris/Shorts pattern pieces* (eliminate pocket pieces)

- Fabric 1—Front (#1), Back #2)

- Fabric 2—Front Waistband (#7), Back Waistband (#8), Tabs (#9), Bottom Ruffle (#10, longer)

- Fabric 3 or pre-gathered lace/eyelet—Bottom Ruffle (#10, shorter)

- Two sash pieces (optional; pattern from Ruffle Dress/Skirt pattern set, piece #7, cut from Fabric 2)

- ½" or ¾" (13mm–19mm) elastic (see Elastic Sizing chart for Vintage Ruffle Capris and Shorts project)

- Four ½"–1" (13mm–3cm) buttons

- Two ½" (13mm) buttons (if using tabs)

- Bodkin or safety pin

- Coordinating thread

*Specific yardage amounts, layout instructons and pattern pieces found on CD in Ruffle Capris and Shorts files.

Make It Just Sew

If you would like to eliminate the pockets from this project, simply modify the pattern as seen in the Banded Bloomer Shorts and Knickers pattern project.

1 Begin with the ruffles. First, make the shorter of the two ruffles. Cut two ruffle pieces for each leg, according to the original pattern, but instead of curving the sides, cut the pieces straight. Sew the two ruffle pieces together at the short ends with right sides together (Fig. A).

   Next, make the longer ruffle. Add 1" (3cm) to the length of the original ruffle pattern piece and cut one piece per leg, but instead of curving the sides, cut the pieces straight so they are the same width as the top (or shorter) ruffle. Sew each longer ruffle piece together at the short ends with right sides together.

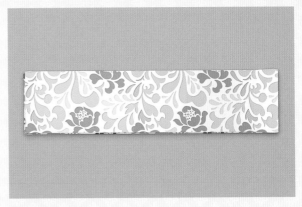

Figure A

2 To hem the four ruffles, fold up the bottom raw edges on each ruffle piece by ½" (13mm) toward the wrong side of the fabric and then another ½" (13mm). Stitch the hem in place.

   Note: You could also finish the bottom edge of both ruffles with a rolled edge done on a serger. If you choose to do this, you may want to reduce both ruffles by ½" (13mm), depending on how much you plan to cut off with your serger.

3 Place the shorter ruffle on top of the longer ruffle, lining up the top, raw edges. Run two rows of gathering stitches through the top of both ruffles. Do this for both sets of ruffles. If you are using a pre-gathered lace or eyelet as your top ruffle, just gather the longer ruffle and cut the pre-gathered trim to measure 1" (3cm) longer than the circumference of the pant legs.

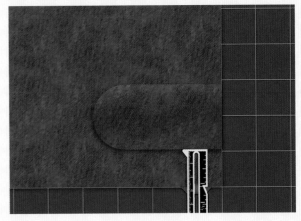

Figure B

Make It Just Sew

If you would like to add the pockets to the Double Ruffle Capris, please refer to the instructions for the Vintage Ruffle Capris and Shorts.

4 To make the side button tabs, cut four tabs. Place two of the tabs with right sides together and sew around the long curved side, leaving the straight, raw edge open. Clip the curves of each tab. Turn to the right side.

5 Sew the front of the pants together with right sides together at the center curved seam. Do the same for the back of the pants. Then sew the front and back of the pants together at the crotch seam with right sides together.

   Insert the sash and the tabs before you sew the side seams of the pants. To make the sash, refer to the Twirl Skirt instructions. For the tab placement, measure up 1" (3cm) from the bottom of each pant leg (Fig. B). Measure down 1" (3cm) along the side seam from the top of the pants for the sash placement. Line up the raw edges of the sash and tabs with the raw edge of the pant front piece. Baste the sash and tab pieces in place. Hand sew buttons on tabs.

Figure C

Figure D

6 Sew down both sides of the pants, catching the tabs and the sash in the ½" (13mm) seam (Fig. C). Turn right side out and press.

7 Attach the ruffles to the bottom of the capris. Gather the ruffles so they are the same circumference as the bottom of the pants. If you are using a pre-gathered lace or eyelet, place your piece right sides together and sew down the short end. Turn right side out. The pre-gathered trim should be the same circumference as the opening in the pants leg. Place the trim on top of the longer ruffle.

Line up the raw edges of the ruffles with the raw edge of the pant leg, right sides together. Pin and sew in place (Fig. D).

8 Press the ruffles down and press the seam up toward the pants. Topstitch or edgestitch around the bottom leg of the pants. Make sure to do this for both pant legs.

9 Attach the waistband as described in steps 12–14 for the Vintage Ruffle Capris and Shorts. Your Double Ruffle Capris are now complete. If you have chosen to insert the optional sash, you can tie it in the front or the back of the pants. It really looks cute both ways!

Pants pictured with Pocket Smock Top (Chapter 1).

CHAPTER THREE

Baby, It's Cold Outside

Classic Dress Coat

My family and I live in the Midwest and it can be pretty chilly here from about October through March, so we spend a lot of time wearing coats. It's always fun for my little ones to have a variety of coats to wear for different occasions. The Classic Dress Coat is a stylish statement piece that every little girl needs in her wardrobe. This coat was created as a great base pattern to which you can add your own personal style and touches. The coat is fully lined with an oversized Peter Pan collar and two sweet pockets on the front. The sleeves can be worn cuffed to reveal the lining fabric.

This coat pairs well with almost all of the pieces in this book and can be made for different types of weather based on the weight of the fabric that you choose. There are so many different options depending on your design aesthetic and climate. Think about using velveteen, denim, wool coating, corduroy or cotton sateen. You could also use quilting-weight cotton for a more lightweight look, but you might consider adding some fusible interfacing to add more structure to the coat if you opt to go that route.

MATERIALS LIST

- ○ Classic Dress Coat pattern pieces* (use Long Coat)
- ○ Optional: Neck Tie (#7) (as seen on Little Lady Coat)
- ○ Fabric 1—Front (#1), Back (#2), Sleeve (#3), Collar (#4), Pocket (#5)
- ○ Fabric 2 (lining)—Front (#1), Back (#2), Collar (#4), Pocket (#5)
- ○ ½"–1" (13mm–3cm) buttons (front)
- ○ Two decorative buttons, any size (pockets)
- ○ Corded piping (collar, optional)
- ○ Ribbon trim (under buttons, optional)
- ○ Coordinating thread

*Specific yardage amounts, layout instructons and pattern pieces found on CD in Classic Dress Coat (Long Coat) files.

Make It Just Sew

If you choose a bold print for this coat, then consider whether or not trim is really necessary in the collar. Sometimes the trim will not really show if the overall print is busy. Just something to think about as you design your handmade creation.

Also pay careful attention to the fabric that you are using for the lining of the pockets. When you fold the pockets down, the lining fabric will, essentially, be upside down. If your fabric is non-directional, it doesn't really matter, but if it is directional, make sure you cut it so that when you fold the pocket down, the print is going in the proper direction.

1 To construct the coat collar, place the two collar pieces right sides together, and sew all the way around the outside curve (Fig. A). If you would like to insert trim or piping into the collar, do so before sewing the collar pieces together according to the Techniques section of the book.

2 Trim the seam of the collar to ⅛" (3mm) using pinking shears. Turn right side out and press. The inside curve of the collar will still be a raw edge.

3 To construct the two pockets, place two of the pocket pieces right sides together and sew all the way around, leaving a 2" (5cm) opening along one of the straight sides that will be sewn to the coat (Fig. B). Clip the corners and curves, turn right side out (through the 2" [5cm] opening) and press. Turn in the seam allowance at the opening and press.

4 Fold the curved corner of the pocket toward the outer fabric according to pattern markings. You can fold over more or less of the pocket depending on the look you are trying to achieve—just remember that the fold is the only part of the pocket that will be left open. Hand- or machine-sew the button to the pocket according to pattern markings. Repeat steps 3 and 4 for the second pocket.

5 Place the pockets on each coat front piece, matching the pattern markings. Pin in place and sew three sides, leaving the folded edge open (Fig. C). Sew reinforcement stitches at the beginning and end of your pocket stitching. (Little ones can be pretty hard on pockets, so you want to make sure the pockets don't rip when they are carrying around all their little treasures or warming up their hands.)

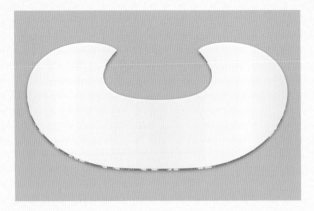

Figure A

Figure B

Figure C

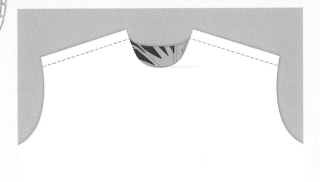

Figure D

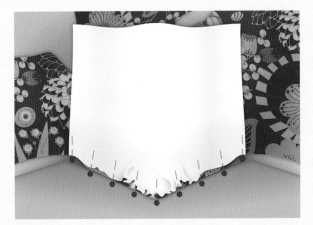

Figure E

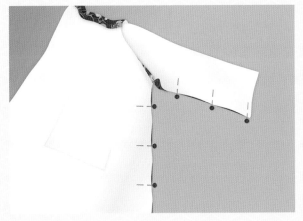

Figure F

6 To construct the exterior of the coat, match the shoulder seams of the back of the coat with the shoulder seams of the front of the coat, right sides together. Sew each shoulder seam in place (Fig. D).

7 To sew the sleeves to the coat, run two rows of gathering stitches between the two markings on the top curve of one sleeve. Gather until the pattern markings line up between the sleeve and the main coat; pin. With right sides together, match the raw edge of the curve of the sleeve with the armhole of the main part of the coat; pin (Fig. E). Sew the sleeve in place. Repeat to attach the other sleeve.

8 Press up a ½" (13mm) hem on each sleeve. Open out the hem.

9 To sew the underarms and sides of the coat, with right sides together, line up the underarm of the sleeve and the sides of the coat. Start pinning at the armpit and work your way out (Fig. F). (That way, if your cutting is off ever so slightly, the armpits will still line up correctly.) Sew down the sleeve to the armpit; pivot your sewing machine foot and continue down the side of the coat to the bottom. Make sure that the ½" (13mm) sleeve hem that you pressed in step 8 is unfolded on both sleeves. Clip a notch in the armpit to remove bulk where the seams come together, being careful not to cut through the stitching.

10 To attach the collar, fold the collar in half to find the center along the neck edge; mark. Find the center back on the coat neckline; mark. Match the center mark of the collar with the center mark of the back of the coat. Start pinning the collar from the center point and work around to the front on each side. Baste the collar in place using a ¼" (6mm) seam allowance.

11 Follow steps 6 through 9 to construct the lining in the same way you constructed the exterior, excluding any pockets.

12 Turn the lining inside out. Put the lining of the coat around the exterior of the coat so that the right sides are together. Line up both front sides of the coat and neck seam; pin in place (Fig G). Sew up one side of the coat front, around the neck and back down the other side of the coat center front. Clip corners and curves around the collar and turn the coat right side out. Tuck the sleeve lining into the outer sleeves. Press the seams, making sure to smooth out the curve around the collar. Press the seam around the neckline toward the lining. To help the collar lay flat, add some understitching on top of the lining fabric close to the seam where the lining and collar come together.

13 To hem the bottom of the coat closed, separate the outer fabric from the lining (Fig. H).

Flip the exterior fabric and the lining fabric toward one another at the side seam so that the right sides are together (Fig. I).

Continue turning the fabrics toward one another until you have formed almost a cocoon around the main part of the coat. (This step may feel a little awkward, but just go with it and trust me—you'll see how this works out.)

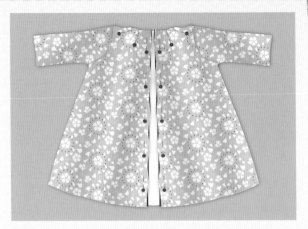

Figure G

Figure H

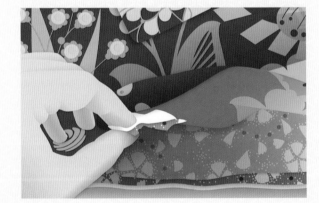

Figure I

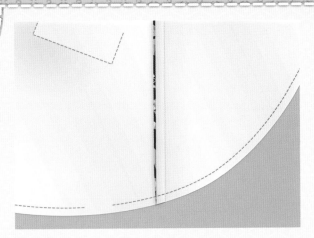

Figure J

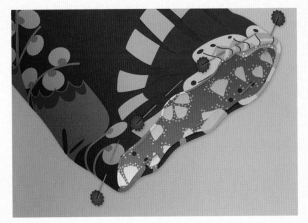

Figure K

14 Sew all the way around the bottom, leaving a 6″(15cm) opening somewhere along the bottom of the coat. Don't leave the opening at the beginning or end—leave it somewhere in the middle (Fig. J). Pull the main part of the coat through the bottom opening. Turn in the seam allowance at the opening and press the bottom hem of the coat. Topstitch along the bottom to close the opening.

15 On each sleeve, turn in the hem along the pressed edge. Turn in the lining hem to match, and pin for each sleeve. Edgestitch around the sleeves (Fig. K).

16 Mark the buttonhole placement according to the pattern markings. Make buttonholes on your machine, and hand-sew or machine-sew your buttons in place.

Make It Just Sew

You can add decorative woven ribbon underneath your buttons if you so choose (refer to the main image). This trim will add some extra detail to your garment that will show when your little lady wears the coat open. It is also a nice little surprise when she takes the coat off.

Classic Dress Coat pictured with Little Lady Coat (next project).

Coat pictured with Banded Shorts (Chapter 2).

Little Lady Coat

The Little Lady Coat is the ultimate sophisticated garment. While it uses the same pattern pieces as the Classic Dress Coat, you'll need to cut the main coat and sleeve at the shorter cutting line.

This coat is classic in style, but has a bit of whimsy with ruffled sleeves and a large neck tie. It looks absolutely adorable paired with the Banded Shorts, Knickers, Ruffle Capris and Shorts, or it can even be worn with jeans for a more casual look.

MATERIALS LIST

- Classic Dress Coat pattern pieces* (use Short Coat)

- Fabric 1—Front (#1), Back (#2), Sleeve (#3), Collar (#4), Pocket (#5)

- Fabric 2 (lining)—Front (#1), Back (#2), Collar (#4), Pocket (#5), Sleeve Ruffle (#6), Tie (#7)

- ½"–1" (13mm–3cm) buttons (front)

- Two decorative buttons, any size (pockets)

- Corded piping (collar, optional)

- Coordinating Thread

*Specific yardage amounts, layout instructons and pattern pieces found on CD in Classic Dress Coat (Short Coat) files.

- -

Make It Just Sew

If you would prefer a non-ruffled sleeve, you can leave off the ruffle for a ¾-length sleeve or use the longer cutting line as you did for the Classic Dress Coat.

- -

1   Construct the coat as you did the Classic Dress Coat, but cut the main piece of the coat at the shorter cutting line. Also use the shorter sleeve cutting line and do not hem the sleeves.

2   To make the sleeve ruffle, fold one ruffle piece in half with right sides together. Match the short, raw edge and sew together (Fig. A). Turn the ruffle right side out. Fold the ruffle in half lengthwise so that the wrong sides are together and the raw edges line up. Run two rows of gathering stitches at ¼" (6mm) and ½" (13mm) along the raw edge of the ruffle. Gather the ruffle until it is the same circumference as the sleeve opening. Do this for both ruffles.

3   Attach the ruffle to the sleeve prior to step 12 in the construction instructions for the Classic Dress Coat. With right sides together, line up the raw edge of the sleeves (exterior only) with the raw edge of the ruffle. The finished edge of the ruffle should be pointing up toward the sleeve. Sew the ruffle to the sleeve making sure to distribute the gathering evenly (Fig. B). Press the ruffles down and press the seam allowance up toward the sleeve of the coat. Attach the lining to the main coat as in step 12 for the Classic Dress Coat, making sure to press a ½" (13mm) hem toward the wrong side of the fabric on both the lining sleeves. Topstitch around the sleeves just above where you attached the ruffle. Now the raw seams of the ruffle will be enclosed in the sleeve.

4   To make the neck sash, cut out two tie pieces. Fold the tie pieces in half lengthwise with right sides together. Sew down the long side to the point, leaving the short, straight side open (Fig. C). Turn right side out and press. Press under the open, raw edge of the tie by ½" (13mm). Edgestitch the raw edge closed. Topstitch the tie, if you so choose.

5   Run two rows of gathering stitches along the short, straight ends of the tie. Gather each piece so that it is approximately 1" (3cm) wide (Fig. D). Attach the gathered end under the collar of the coat at the shoulder seam. Sew it to the coat as close to the collar as possible, using a ¼" (6mm) seam allowance. (Tie the neck tie in a large knot in the center of the coat front after you have put it on your child.)

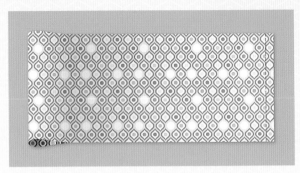

Figure A

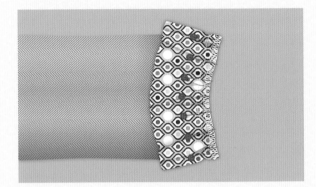

Figure B

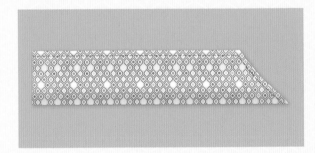

Figure C

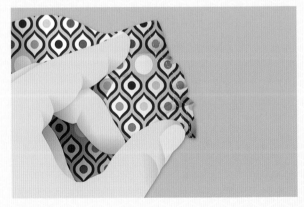

Figure D

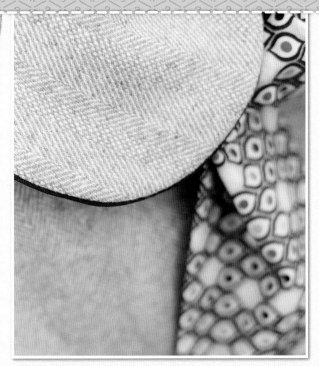

Coat pictured with Banded Shorts (Chapter 2).

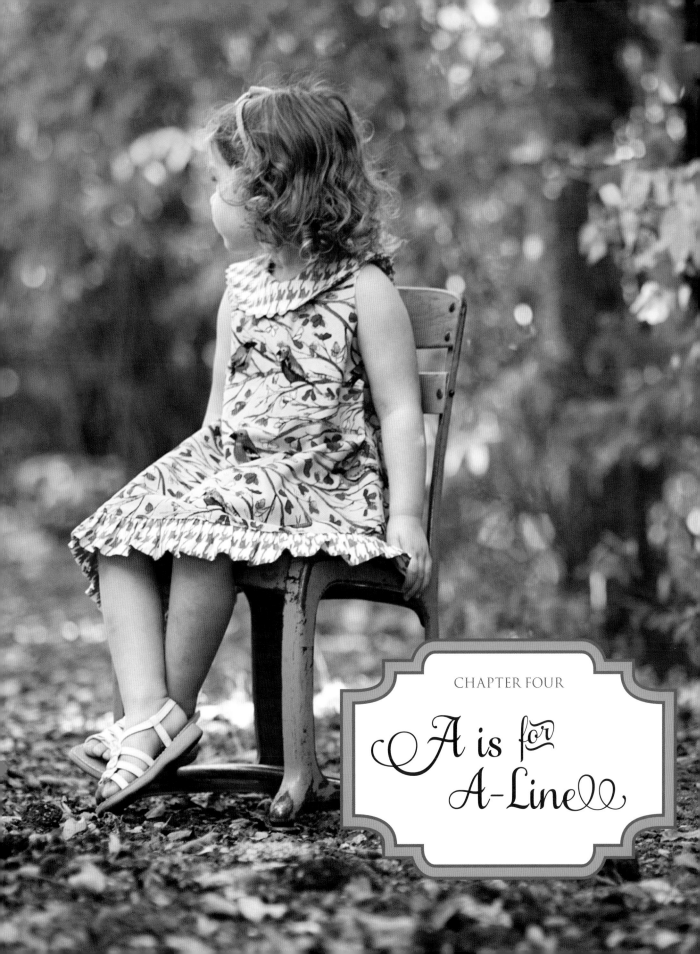

CHAPTER FOUR

A is for A-Line

Dress/Top pictured with Vintage Ruffle Capris (Chapter 2).

Classic A-Line Dress or Top

THERE IS SOMETHING SO SWEET yet practical about a traditional A-line style dress. It is an easy silhouette for girls of all shapes and sizes to wear, and can be dressed up or down depending on the occasion. When I want to whip up a quick dress for one of my girls, this is my go-to pattern. Once you learn how this dress is constructed, you are going to want to make this time and time again.

A-LINE STYLE DRESSES ARE PERFECT for layering, so they can take your child throughout the different seasons. You can layer them with a long-sleeved T-shirt, tights, leggings, jeans or wear a cardigan on top. A dress and top cutting length have been provided so you have the option to make either length with any variation. Also, the pattern design is generous in the sense that even if your little one grows out of the length of her dress, it will still fit as an adorable top.

ALL OF THE DESIGN OPTIONS for the traditional A-line are so exciting! You can make it simple, add embellishments, piping and trim, change the collar, add a ruffle at the hem, add long sleeves and so much more. The A-line dresses in this book are fully lined for complete comfort. After you sew this dress, I hope you are as excited about the A-line style as I am.

MATERIALS LIST

❍ Classic A-Line Dress pattern pieces* (bib optional, eliminate collar)

❍ Fabric 1—Front and Back (#1)

❍ Fabric 2—Front and Back (#1), Bib (#5, optional)

❍ One ½"–1" (13mm–3cm) button

❍ Double-sided fusible interfacing (bib, optional)

❍ Decorative trim, buttons (bib, optional)

❍ Coordinating thread

*Specific yardage amounts, layout instructons and pattern pieces found on CD in Classic A-Line Dress files.

Make It Just Sew

The A-line dress is intended to fall just above the knee. If you have a tall little lady, I would suggest cutting a longer length, while maintaining the proper size in the rest of the garment. Or consider adding the 2" (5cm) ruffle as seen in later variations.

The top shown here has a sweet pre-gathered eyelet trim poking out at the bottom of the top. To add the trim, baste it to the exterior of the top/dress prior to step 11, or (if you don't mind seeing part of it on the underside of the garment) add the trim at the end.

1 For the optional bib embellishment, apply double-sided fusible interfacing to the wrong side of the fabric intended for the bib (follow manufacturer's instructions). Make sure your fabric is large enough to accommodate the bib pattern piece. Trace the bib pattern piece on the paper side of the interfacing and cut out the bib. Remove the paper backing and use your iron to fuse the bib to the dress front at the marks (Fig. A).

2 The bib can be embellished with many different types of trim. Consider using rickrack, pre-gathered eyelet, fabric ruffles, picot edging or bias tape. You can pin the trim around the edge of the bib or you can use Wash-A-Way Wonder Tape to stick the trim to the edge of the bib. Sew trim around the edge of the bib. If you plan to sew any buttons on the bib, do so at this time (Fig. B).

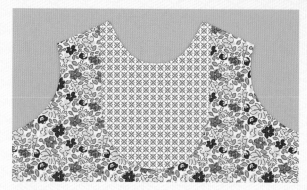

Figure A

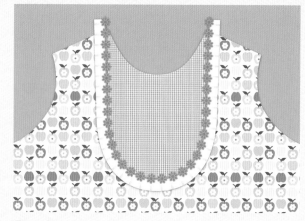

Figure B

Make It Just Sew

When using trim around a curved edge, use your iron to press your trim in the direction of the curve. This will help the trim to lay nicely around the curve. This is a technique that works great for piping, rickrack and pre-gathered trims, as well as bias binding.

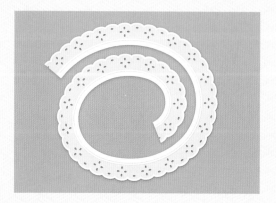

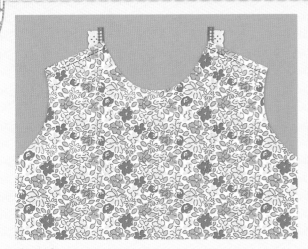

Figure C

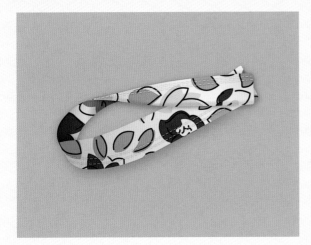

Figure D

3 Begin the dress by finding the center of the back of the dress and the lining by folding each piece in half and marking the neck edge. Cut a slit down the back of the dress and the lining—about 3"–5" (8cm–13cm) long, depending on dress size. (Cut a smaller slit for smaller sizes and a larger slit for larger sizes.)

4 Match the front of the dress with the back of the dress, right sides together, and sew across both shoulder seams. Do this for the exterior and lining pieces (Fig. C).

5 To make the back button closure, cut a piece of fabric 1" (3cm) wide by 3" (8cm) long. Cut this piece longer if you're using a very large button; cut it shorter if you are using a tiny button. The loop needs to be able to go around the button, but you also don't want it to be so large that it will slip off.

Just as you have done when making bias tipe, fold the button loop piece in half lengthwise and press. Fold each long edge in to the center and press. Sew as close to the edge of the fabric as possible. Now fold the piece in half widthwise, matching the two short edges and creating a twist so the top side of both ends is up (as shown). Baste the short edges to hold them in place. You have now formed your loop closure (Fig. D).

6 To baste the loop closure to the back exterior of the dress, measure down ¾" (19mm) from the neck edge on the back of the dress and mark. Line up the raw edge of the loop with the raw edge of the right side of the slit in the back of the dress at the mark. Baste the loop in place (Fig. E).

7 With right sides together, match the neck hole opening and the back slit. Start stitching ½" (13mm) below the center of the slit of the dress and lining. Stitch up one side of the slit, around the neckline, and back down to a ½" (13mm) below the slit, meeting your starting stitches (Fig. F).

8 Clip the corners and curves, and cut all the way down, almost to the stitching in the back slit. If you don't cut close enough to the stitches, your dress will not turn right side out properly. Cut almost down to the stitches, just don't cut through them.

Turn right side out and press, making sure to smooth out the curve in the neckline and the slit. If the slit does not lay flat, you may not have cut far enough down. Turn the dress inside out again and cut farther down.

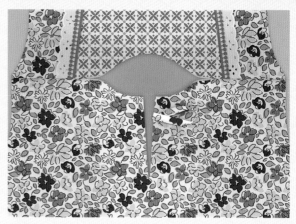
Figure E

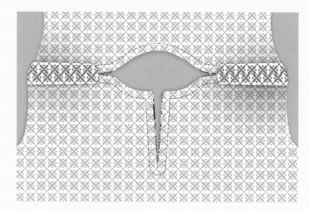
Figure F

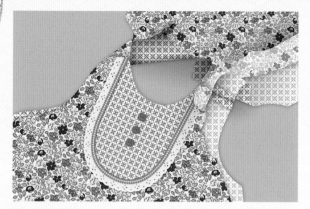

Figure G

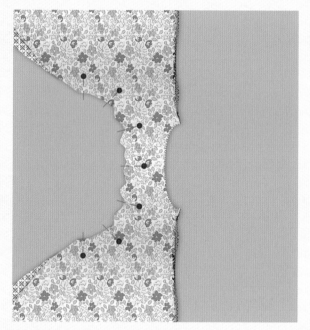

Figure H

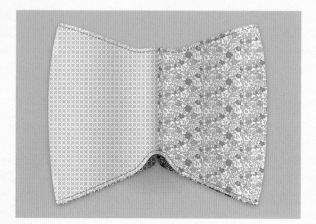

Figure I

9 Lay out the dress in front of you, with either the dress side up or the lining side up (it does not matter). Separate the dress fabric from the lining fabric on one side of the dress (Fig. G).

If the dress side is right side up, then do the following: Pull the dress fabric over the top of the dress and pull the lining fabric under the dress to the other side. You are doing this in order to have the right sides of the armholes facing each other. When you have pulled the exterior side over and the lining side under (think over, under), line up the armholes with right sides together, wrapping the other armhole of the dress into what looks like a cocoon. Pin in place, sew the armhole and clip the curve (Fig. H).

10 After you have sewn the armhole, pull the dress through the cocoon-like tube so that it turns. Just keep pulling until it flips right side out. Once it's out, press the curve of the armhole. Repeat steps 8 and 9 for the other armhole, going over to the opposite side.

11 Separate the lining fabric from the dress fabric. With the dress in front of you and the lining to the opposite side, match the raw edges of the lining to the lining and dress to dress, right sides together (Fig. I). Pin the sides of the dress, starting at the armpit where the seams all come together, and work your way down both sides. (The reason for this is so that if your cutting was off ever so slightly, the armholes will still match up nicely.)

Sew down both sides of the dress: Start at the bottom, sew up to the armpit, pivot your presser foot and sew back down the other side. Clip out the bulk by the armpit where all seams come together; just make sure you don't cut through the stitches. Turn the dress right side out and press the side seams open.

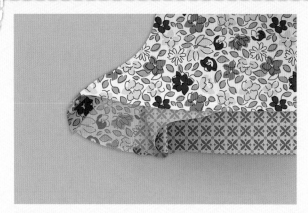

Figure J

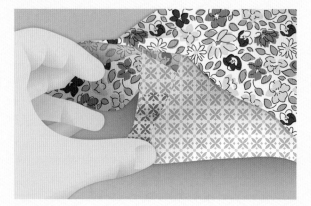

Figure K

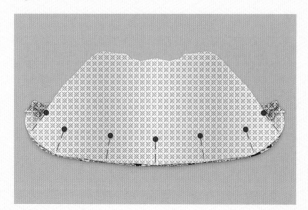

Figure L

12 Hem the bottom of the dress. This step will feel complicated, but it's really not. Once you understand how this works, you will want to finish all of your lined garments this way. Lay your dress out in front of you. Separate the dress fabric from the lining fabric at one of the side seams (right now the dress and lining fabrics are wrong sides together) (Fig. J).

Turn (or twist) the side seams toward one another so that the right sides of the fabric are together. Do this by turning the dress seam one direction and the lining seam the opposite direction. Place the exterior in your left hand and the lining in your right hand. Turn the exterior toward the right and the interior to the left so the right sides are together. Do this only on one side of the dress (Fig. K). Remember, only turn the side seams that are right next to each other; do not bring one side seam over the top of the dress to the other side (a common mistake).

Once you have turned the immediate side seams so that right sides are together, pin them in place. Continue to turn the dress and pin the right sides together (Fig. L). You will form sort of a cocoon around the top of the dress. Sew along the bottom of the dress, leaving a 4" (10cm) opening in the bottom. This might seem very awkward or wrong, but just go with it and you will see.

13 When you have sewn along the bottom of the dress, it will look like a jumbled mess. Pull the main part of the dress through the 4" (10cm) opening to turn right side out. Press the seams open. Press under the 4" (10cm) section that you left open so that it lines up with the rest of the hem of the dress, and topstitch along the bottom of the dress. The topstitching will close the opening.

14 Sew a button to the back of the dress.

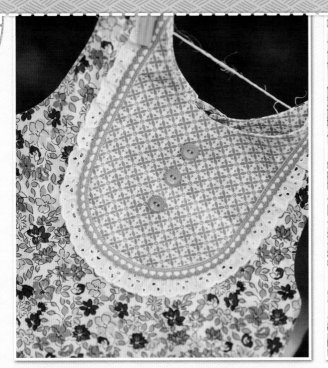

Dress/top pictured with Vintage Ruffle Capris (Chapter 2).

Make It Just Sew

If steps 12 and 13 make you nervous, you can press under ½ "(13mm) each of the lining fabric and exterior fabric, both toward the wrong side, to hem the dress. Then, topstitch the two layers together. Or you can hem them as two separate layers using ¼"(6mm) traditional hem for the exterior fabric and a ¼ " (6mm) and ½ " (13mm) hem for the lining. That said, I would encourage you to try steps 12 and 13, as it is a much easier way to finish the hem of a lined garment.

Round Neck A-Line Dress

The Round Neck A-Line Dress was inspired by the fashion trends of the 1960s and is another way to change up the Classic A-Line Dress. It has a ruffle added to the hem for added length.

This dress offers a fun way to use several coordinating prints. I would suggest using a smaller-scale print for the collar and the ruffle and trying a medium- or large-scale print for the main part of the dress. The collar can be trimmed out with rickrack, piping, loopy trim or any other trim that you think would work well within a seam.

MATERIALS LIST

- ○ Classic A-Line Dress pattern pieces*
- ○ Fabric 1—Front and Back (#1)
- ○ Fabric 2—Front and Back (#1), Bottom Ruffle (#2), Collar (#7)
- ○ One ½"–1" (13mm–3cm) button (back)
- ○ Rickrack or other trim (collar)
- ○ Coordinating thread

*Specific yardage amounts, layout instructons and pattern pieces found on CD in Classic A-Line Dress files.

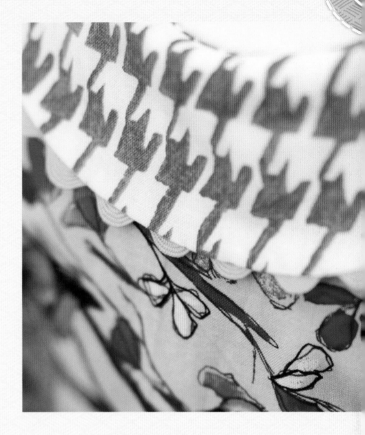

Make It Just Sew

The round neck on the Round Neck A-Line Dress is another perfect spot for some embellishment. Consider adding a hand-sewn yo-yo with a covered button in the center. Or if you have machine embroidery on your machine, this would be a wonderful spot for a monogram. And finally, don't forget about the beauty of hand embroidery. This round neck collar would look beautiful with some hand-embroidered flowers or even several rows of simple multi-colored running stitches.

If you would like to use a different closure on the back of the dress, try using a good-quality elastic hairband instead of the loop closure. Just make sure you sew over it several times since it is elastic and can have a tendency to pull out your stitches if not secured properly.

1 Begin with the collar. If you would like to add rickrack in the collar, do so prior to sewing the two collar pieces together. Line up the trim with the edge of the collar, or adjust as needed depending on your trim size. Baste the trim to one of the collar pieces (Fig. A).

Place the collar pieces right sides together and sew along the long outer curve, leaving the inner curve and short ends open (Fig. B). Clip the curves, turn right side out and press.

2 Complete steps 1 and 2 from the Classic A-Line Dress. Match the collar to the neckline edge, matching the shoulder seam marks. The two short ends of the collar should extend beyond the back slit of the dress.

3 Baste the collar to the exterior of the dress, sewing along the neckline and down the two short ends.

4 Continue with steps 3–11 of the Classic A-Line Dress. Stop prior to step 12 and finish the dress according to the following steps.

5 Cut the ruffle pieces and sew them together at the short ends, right sides together. You now have a circular band of fabric. With wrong sides together, fold the ruffle fabric in half, lengthwise, lining up the raw edges.

6 Run two rows of gathering stitches along the raw edge of the ruffle. Gather the fabric until the ruffle is the same circumference as the bottom of the dress.

7 Line up the raw edges of the dress and lining fabric with the raw edge of the ruffle. At this point the finished edge of the ruffle should point up toward the main part of the dress. Sew the ruffle to the dress. Finish the raw edge with pinking shears, a tight zigzag stitch or a serger. Press the ruffle down away from the dress and press the seam allowance up toward the dress. Topstitch along the bottom edge of the dress.

8 Sew a button to the back of the dress.

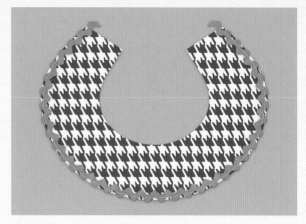

Figure A

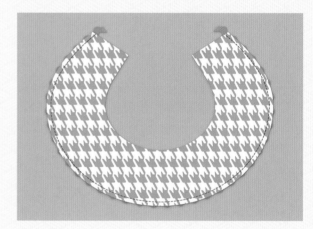

Figure B

Make It Just Sew

If you prefer to have no seams showing on the underside of the finished dress, line up the raw edge of the ruffle with the raw edge of the dress (the finished edge of the ruffle should point up toward the dress) and baste the ruffle to the exterior of the dress. Make sure you do not stitch it to the lining of the dress. Press a ½" (13mm) hem on the interior dress lining toward the wrong side of the fabric. Place the exterior dress with ruffle together with the lining and run a row of topstitching toward the bottom of the dress. This will encase the ruffle so you will have no exposed seams on the interior of the garment.

Ruffle Sleeve A-Line Dress

THOUGH THE CLASSIC A-LINE IS a great dress for layering, sometimes your little one may prefer a long-sleeved dress especially for dressier, cooler weather occasions. That's when the Ruffle Sleeve A-Line comes out to play.

YOU CAN CONSTRUCT THIS DRESS with or without the embellished bib and with or without the round collar. Or you could eliminate the ruffle on the sleeve completely for a ¾-length sleeve. The options and combinations are endless. Many of the techniques used for the Ruffle Sleeve A-Line Dress are ones that you have used or will use with the other patterns throughout this book.

MATERIALS LIST

- ○ Classic A-Line Dress pattern pieces*
- ○ Fabric 1—Front and Back (#1), Sleeve (#3)
- ○ Fabric 2—Front and Back (#1), Sleeve (#3), Sleeve Ruffle (#4), Monogram (#6, optional)
- ○ One ½"–1" (13mm–3cm) button (back)
- ○ Two ½" (13mm) buttons (monogram, optional)
- ○ Coordinating thread

*Specific yardage amounts, layout instructons and pattern pieces found on CD in Classic A-Line Dress files.

Make It Just Sew

The Ruffle Sleeve A-Line Dress is a great dress to use a more bold patterned fabric. You can also choose to add a different patterned fabric for the sleeves. If you decide to go with three patterned fabrics (one for the main dress, one for the sleeves and one for the ruffle and optional interchangeable monogram), just make sure you think about pattern scale and placement when creating your special garment.

You can also add some additional interest by adding your favorite trim at the hem or in the seam between the ruffles and the main sleeve.

1 Construct the Ruffle Sleeve A-Line Dress in the same manner as the Classic A-Line Dress following steps 3–6.

2 To add the sleeves, refer to steps 7–9 from the Classic Dress Coat. Do this for both the exterior fabric and the lining of the dress. There is no need to press the ½" (13mm) sleeve hem on the exterior fabric, but make sure you do for the lining fabric and then unfold it.

3 Attach the ruffle to the sleeve of the exterior of the dress in the same manner as step 2 for the Little Lady Coat.

4 Once you have attached the ruffle to the sleeve, sew the exterior of the dress to the lining. Turn the lining of the dress inside out and line up the neckline so that the right sides of the exterior and lining are facing one another. Sew from ½" (13mm) below the back slit, up around the neckline and back down to ½" (13mm) below the slit, just as you did in step 7 for the Classic A-Line Dress. Clip the corners and curves, making sure to clip all the way down to the stitching (but not through it) in the center back slit. Turn right side out, tuck lining sleeves into exterior sleeves and press.

5 Fold the hem of the sleeve lining back up. Run a row of topstitching on the sleeve using a ¼" (6mm) seam allowance. This will attach the sleeve lining to the exterior sleeve and will fully encase the ruffle seam.

6 Finish the dress hem following steps 11–13 for the Classic A-Line Dress. Again, if this finishing technique makes you nervous, you have a couple other options. You can fold a ½" (13mm) up toward the wrong side of the fabric of both the lining and the exterior and then topstitch them together. Or, leave them as two separate pieces and fold them both ¼" (6mm) toward the wrong side of the fabric and then hem the lining up another ½" (13mm) and the exterior fabric another ¼" (6mm). This will make it so that the dress exterior and the dress lining are two separate pieces. I hope you will try the original technique, but I want to provide you with other options, just in case.

Make It Just Sew: Add Interchangeable Monograms

I absolutely adore monograms. Machine embroidery is such a wonderful way to personalize garments and make them truly one of a kind. However, if you have several little girls in your family, you may be hesitant to monogram a dress front due to the fact that you hope to pass it down to a younger sibling. I know how that goes. Many of the dresses I create for my oldest daughter, Savannah, eventually end up with Matilda, but I think monograms are so classic and beautiful. I wanted to figure out a way to personalize my children's clothing in a nonpermanent way.

The interchangeable monogram can be used in several different ways. It is double sided, so you can have one of your girls' monograms on one side and your other child's monogram on the other side. That way when the older one grows out of the garment, you can simply flip the monogram over and it's ready for your younger child.

While I sometimes hesitate making a garment for a specific holiday as it's only worn a handful of times, I think it's fun for kids to have special things for the holidays. So think about doing this: Construct a fairly neutral A-line style dress and create a bunch of different interchangeable pieces for different holidays or occasions! Perhaps an apple for back to school, a pumpkin for Halloween or Thanksgiving, an ornament for Christmas, hearts for Valentine's Day and so on. If you have embroidery capabilities on your sewing machine, you could go wild with all the possibilities. But if you don't, you can certainly create hand-embroidered interchangeable pieces ,which is such a gorgeous, loving, handmade touch.

The interchangeable monogram pictured on this page was designed to go with the Classic A-Line Dress; however, you could certainly add it to the Sweet Dress, Dainty Darling Dress or Play Frock. You will just have to decide where you would like to place it on each of the other garments.

To make the monogram tab, machine- or hand-embroider initials or designs on fabric. Cut two monogram tab pattern pieces out of the fabric, making sure to center the embroidery design. Place the monogram tab pieces with right sides together and sew all the way around the tab, leaving a 2" (5cm) opening on one of the straight edges. Turn the tab right side out and press, pressing the opening edges under so they align with the rest of the tab's edge. Edgestitch all the way around the tab to close the opening. Machine sew buttonholes on the tab according to the pattern markings. Hand- or machine-sew buttons to the dress the same width apart as the monogram tab. Button the monogram tab to the dress.

CHAPTER FIVE

Sugar, Spice and Everything Nice

The Sweet Dress

There's something about a large bow tied around the waist of a little girl's dress that just says special and fancy. The Sweet Dress has everything you and your little girl could hope for in a dress—a gathered skirt, a large sash and a Peter Pan collar. Does it get any sweeter than that? I don't think so. But wait until you see your little lady wearing this dress; it takes the cuteness factor to a whole new level!

There are so many different ways to embellish the skirt on this dress. Consider using a coordinating fabric like a ribbon. You could also add rickrack or loopy trim poking out at the skirt hem. The options are endless; the fabric selection and details will make your garment truly unique.

MATERIALS LIST

- ❍ The Sweet Dress pattern pieces*
  (use double-layer skirt pieces)

- ❍ Fabric 1—Bodice Front (#1), Bodice Back (#2)

- ❍ Fabric 2—Skirt (#6, upper skirt)

- ❍ Fabric 3—Skirt (#6, under skirt), Center Sash (#8),
  Sash Tie Ends (#9)

- ❍ Fabric 4—Collar (#10)

- ❍ ½"–1" (13mm–3cm) buttons (back)

- ❍ Corded piping (collar and underarms, optional)

- ❍ Coordinating thread

*Specific yardage amounts, layout instructons and pattern pieces found on CD in The Sweet Dress files.

Make It Just Sew

If you would like to add piping into the armholes, baste it in place prior to step 6. Refer to the Techniques section of the book for a refresher on piping.

Likewise, if you are not using the waist sash and would prefer to add piping into the waist seam, do so prior to step 10 by basting your piping to the bodice.

1 To construct the sash, there are three pieces: one center piece and two side pieces. With right sides together, sew the two side sash pieces to the center piece along the short ends.

With right sides together, fold the long sash piece in half lengthwise (Fig. A). Sew along both short ends, and from one end to the other, leaving a 3" (8cm) opening in the middle of the long side. Clip the corners, turn the sash right side out and press, making sure to press out the corners nicely. Topstitch the sash to close the opening or use a slipstitch or whipstitch to close the opening by hand.

2 Next, construct the collar. If you will be adding piping or rickrack into the collar, do so at this time. (Refer to the Techniques section on piping instructions.) Place the two collar pieces right sides together and sew all the way around the outer curve. Use pinking shears to trim the seam allowance down to ⅛" (3mm) (Fig. B). Turn right side out and press. The inner curve should still be open and have a raw edge. Do this for both collar pieces.

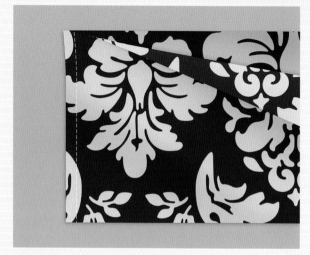

Figure A

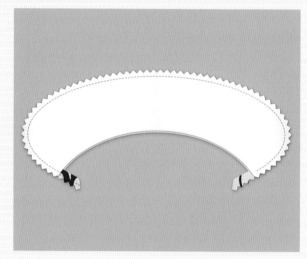

Figure B

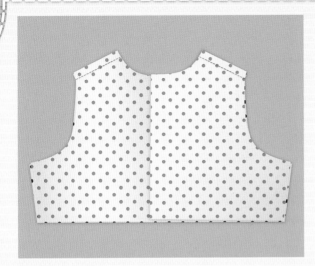

Figure C

Figure D

3 With right sides together, sew the front bodice piece to the back bodice pieces at the shoulder seams. Do this for the exterior bodice pieces and the lining bodice pieces (Fig. C).

4 Starting in the very center of the bodice front, slightly overlap the edge of the two collar pieces. This will ensure that, once you've sewn in the lining, the collar will come together nicely in the center. Baste the collar to the dress bodice. Please note, you will need to ease in the collar a little bit to have it fit around the neck opening.

5 Place the exterior bodice and the lining bodice right sides together. Sew up the back of the bodice, around the neck and back down the other side (Fig. D). Sew the underarms as well. Clip the corners and curves, turn right side out and press.

6 Sew the sides of the bodice. (Again, this is the same technique as used with the Classic A-Line Dress.) Pull apart the exterior and lining bodice fabrics and place them right sides together. Sew down the right and then the left side. Clip a notch under the armpits to remove any bulk and press. Do this for both sides. Refer to the Classic A-Line Dress for more detailed instruction on finishing side seams after completing a lined armhole.

7 Make buttonholes on the back of the bodice according to pattern markings. Use a seam ripper to open buttonholes and finish with an anti-fray product. Machine- or hand-sew buttons to the opposite side according to pattern markings. Button the bodice back and baste stitch the very bottom of the bodice where the two sides of the bodice overlap.

8 Place the two shorter skirt pieces with right sides together and sew together at the two short sides. Hem the skirt by pressing up ½" (13mm) toward the wrong side of the fabric and then another ½" (13mm) toward the wrong side of the fabric, and sew in place using a ½" (13mm) seam allowance. If you are making a double-layer skirt, do the same for the longer skirt piece. Also, if you would like to add trim to the bottom of the skirt, now would be the time to do so.

If you are making a double-layer skirt, place the longer skirt piece underneath the shorter skirt piece, lining up the top, raw edge and side seams. Baste stitch the two skirt pieces together.

9 Run two rows of gathering stitches all the way around the top of the skirt a ¼" (6mm) and ½" (13mm) away from the raw edge. Pull the threads and gather the skirt until it is the same circumference as the bottom edge of the bodice (Fig. E). Turn the skirt inside out and, with right sides together, line up the raw edge of the skirt with the raw edge of the bodice and the side seams. The bodice will be inside the skirt. Sew the skirt to the bodice, making sure to keep the gathers evenly spaced. Press the seam up toward the bodice. Finish the edge with a serger or zigzag stitch.

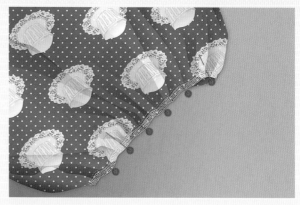

Figure E

10 If you want the sash to be permanently attached to the dress, run two rows of gathering stitches in the side seam of the sash. Do this on both sides. Gather the sides of the sash as much as possible, making the sash approximately 2"–3" (5cm–8cm) wide. Line up the side seam of the sash and the side seam of the bodice (Fig. F). Sew on top of both seams to attach the sash.

You can also make two loops and thread the sash instead of permanently attaching it to the dress. Make the loops in the same way as for the back button loop closure for the Classic A-Line Dress. Sew the loops to the side seams of the bodice.

Figure F

Dainty Darling Dress

PRECIOUS. THAT'S WHAT EVERYONE WILL be saying when your sweet girl is wearing the Dainty Darling Dress. When I see pictures of children's wear from the late 1940s, 1950s and early 1960s, puff sleeves were all the rage and I can definitely see why. There is nothing that says "classic little girl" more than a puff sleeve. It is the epitome of dainty sweetness.

THIS DRESS IS CONSTRUCTED IN the same manner as The Sweet Dress, but you will omit finishing the armholes. Also, this piece only has a single-layer skirt made from the shorter skirt piece. If you would prefer to add the double-layer skirt, by all means, go for it!

MATERIALS LIST

- ❍ The Sweet Dress pattern pieces* (use upper skirt cutting lines)
- ❍ Fabric 1—Bodice Front (#1), Bodice Back (#2)
- ❍ Fabric 2—Sleeve (#3), Skirt (#6, upper skirt)
- ❍ Fabric 3—Sleeve Band (#4), Center Sash (#8), Sash Tie Ends (#9)
- ❍ Fabric 4—Collar (#10)
- ❍ ½"–1" (13mm–3cm) buttons (back)
- ❍ Corded piping (collar, optional)
- ❍ Coordinating thread

*Specific yardage amounts, layout instructons and pattern pieces found on CD in The Sweet Dress files.

Make It Just Sew

The Dainty Darling Dress offers you a great place to practice your hand-sewing skills. While I am not opposed to machine stitching and topstitching on most children's garments, the puff sleeves are one of the few places where hand sewing is a must. You can use a whipstitch, slipstitch or blind stitch, but whichever stitch you choose, make sure it doesn't show through to the exterior side of your garment.

Also, to make sure your Peter Pan collar meets perfectly in the center of the bodice, overlap the two ends in the center of the bodice ever so slightly (about ¼"[6mm]) when basting your collar in place to the exterior of the fabric.

1   Complete steps 1–5 for The Sweet Dress, but don't sew the armholes.

2   Make the sleeve binding for the puff sleeve. Along the long edges of each sleeve band, fold in ¼" (6mm) to the wrong side; press. Fold the bands in half again and press.

3   To make the puff sleeves, gather the sleeves along the straight edge between the pattern markings. Open out the sleeve band and, with right sides together, line up the raw edge of the band piece with the raw, straight edge of the sleeve (Fig. A). Sew the band to the sleeve along the ¼" (6mm) fold.

Fold the sleeve in half, right sides together, matching the underarm seam. With the sleeve band completely unfolded, sew the seam (Fig. B). Fold the sleeve binding over to the wrong side of the sleeve and slipstitch in place.

4   Skip step 6 from The Sweet Dress. You will add puff sleeves, so you don't need to finish the armholes. With right sides together, stitch the side seams of both the bodice and the bodice lining sections.

5   To add the puff sleeves to the bodice, run two rows of gathering stitches between the two dots on the cap of both sleeves. Gather until they line up with the bodice armhole markings. With the bodice inside out and right sides together, pin the raw edge of the sleeve to the raw edge of the armhole. The sleeve will now be inside the bodice (Fig. C). Sew all the way around the sleeve. Finish the raw edge with pinking shears, a tight zigzag stitch or a serger.

6   Complete the rest of the Dainty Darling Dress by following steps 7–10 of The Sweet Dress instructions.

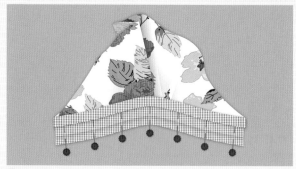

Figure A

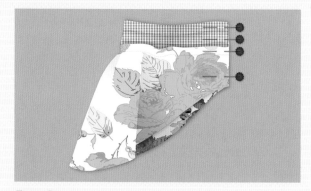

Figure B

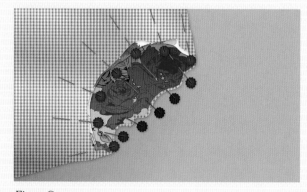

Figure C

Make It Just Sew

Consider adding trim in the seam between the sleeve and the sleeve binding to add additional detail to the dress. Use the same trim at the hem of the dress and/ or in the collar seem to create one cohesive look.

Sweet Bib Ruffle Dress

The Sweet Bib Ruffle Dress is a combination of many different dresses that all come together in this one adorable ensemble. This dress has an embellished bib front as well as a whimsical ruffle added to the bottom of the dress skirt.

This dress variation offers you many ways to incorporate your favorite fabrics and trims. Consider getting creative by mixing and matching different fabric weights such as a lightweight corduroy, woven cotton, velveteen, seersucker or twill.

MATERIALS LIST

- ○ The Sweet Dress pattern pieces*
- ○ Fabric 1—Bodice Front (#1), Bodice Back (#2)
- ○ Fabric 2—Skirt (#6, ruffle skirt)
- ○ Fabric 3—Bib (#5), Bottom Ruffle (#7)
- ○ ½"–1" (13mm–3cm) buttons (back)
- ○ Trim and button embellishment (bib)
- ○ Corded piping (underarms, optional)
- ○ Coordinating thread

*Specific yardage amounts, layout instructons and pattern pieces found on CD in The Sweet Dress files.

Make It Just Sew

When making this dress, you can adjust the bib pattern piece any way you would like. You can have a large bib that will take up a good portion of the bodice front or you can move the piece and have it take up a smaller portion. That design decision is up to you.

Although this dress doesn't have a sash, you can use a sash piece from any variation in this chapter if you'd like to add one. Simply attach the sash as you would for The Sweet Dress.

1 Attach the bib to the bodice front in the same manner as the Classic A-Line Dress embellished bib option. Trim off any excess bib piece that is out of line with the top of the bodice. Add your selected trim around the edge of the bodice and hand-sew or machine-sew buttons to the front (Fig. A).

2 Construct the dress in the same manner as The Sweet Dress, but omit the sash and use the shorter skirt piece. Do not hem the skirt because you will be adding a ruffle to the bottom edge.

3 Make the lower ruffle. With right sides together, sew the ruffle pieces together at the short ends. Once you've sewn all the pieces together, you will have a circular piece of fabric. With wrong sides together, fold the ruffle in half lengthwise and press.

4 Run two rows of gathering stitches and gather the ruffle along the raw edges through both layers. Pull the threads until the ruffle is the same circumference as the bottom of the dress skirt.

5 After you have sewn the main skirt pieces together at the side seams, add the ruffle to the bottom of the skirt. Line up the raw edge of the bottom of the skirt with the raw edge of the ruffle, right sides together, and sew in place. Press the seam up toward the skirt, and topstitch around the bottom of the skirt. This is very similar to how you added the ruffle to the sleeve of the Little Lady Coat or to the bottom of the Round Neck A-Line Dress.

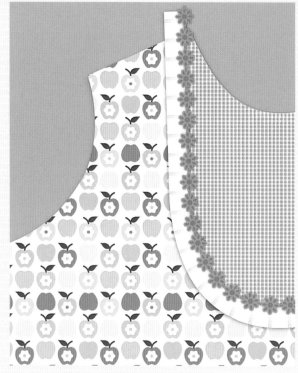

Figure A

- -

Make It Just Sew

The seam between the skirt and the ruffle would be a great place to add trim such as rickrack. Baste your trim to the bottom of the skirt prior to adding the ruffle. Or you could add trim on top of the seam after you have sewn the ruffle to the skirt and omit the topstitching. Piping could be added into the waist seam of this dress as well, if you don't use a waist sash.

- -

Make It Just Sew: Variation

The Sweet Dress pattern offers you unlimited design possibilities. The pictured variation shows the pattern with striped piping around the neckline and in the armholes. Also, it is a single-layer skirt with a loopy trim poking out the bottom of the skirt and a woven trim attached to the bottom of the dress for an added special touch.

CHAPTER SIX

The

Finishing Touch

Embellished Bib Shirt

Embellished shirts are a great way to round out your child's wardrobe. Yes, you could definitely make your own T-shirts, but sometimes it's just not worth the time—especially when you can take a readymade T-shirt and give it a handmade look!

There are so many options for embellishing the bib on this shirt, so be creative. I have a soft spot for rickrack, but you can use just about any trim you'd like. Also, you don't have to use cotton for appliqué; consider using textured fabrics like velveteen, corduroy or chenille. Additionally, think about adding a ruffle or other pre-gathered trim layered at the top of your T-shirt for a custom boutique-style look.

MATERIALS LIST

○ Bib pattern piece* (from Finishing Touches pattern pieces set)

○ 1 T-shirt

○ 1 fat quarter of fabric—Bib

○ Double-sided fusible web

○ ½–¾ yard (0.5m–0.7m) rickrack or other trim

○ Coordinating thread

*Pattern piece found on CD in Finishing Touches files.

1 Trace the bib pattern piece onto double-sided fusible web and cut out. Cut the pattern piece from your fabric as well.

2 Line up the edge of the rickrack with the curved edge of the bib. Sew the rickrack to the bib by stitching down the center of the trim (Fig. A). Clip the curves of the bib, including the rickrack. Press rickrack toward the wrong side of the fabric. Half of the rickrack should be poking out from the edge of the bib.

3 Place the bib on top of the t-shirt front matching the neckline edge. Trim the bib edge as necessary to match the t-shirt. Press under the top edge of the bib by approximately ¼"(6mm) to the wrong side of the fabric.

4 Apply the double-sided fusible web to the wrong side of the bib according to manufacturer's directions. Once one side is fused, remove the remaining paper and position the bib on your T-shirt. Move it around until it's centered on the shirt and looks pleasing to you. Once you are happy with the position of the bib, fuse it to the shirt with your iron. Secure in place by edgestitching around the entire bib. Finish with decorative buttons if you so choose.

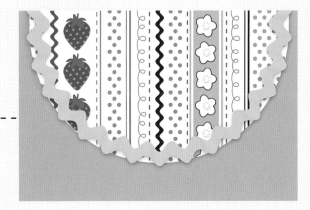

Figure A

Make It Just Sew

Make sure you use double-sided fusible web to apply your bib. Many types of fusible web only fuse on one side or are intended to be sewn into a garment, which is not what you want for this project. Some popular double-sided brands include Steam-A-Seam Lite and Wonder-Under.

Typically with appliqué, you cut out a square of fabric larger than your pattern piece, apply double-sided fusible web to the wrong side of the fabric, trace your pattern piece, then cut it out and fuse it to your other fabric. For this bib, you will be doing things a little differently to accommodate the rickrack trim.

Fabric-Covered Button Headband

Fabric-covered buttons are on my list of top five favorite embellishments for children's clothing. I think they add a really special finishing touch to garments, lending them a little extra charm.

Covered buttons don't have to be reserved strictly for garments; they can be used as accessories as well. Try using different sized covered buttons to create a custom headband for your little lady to bring her whole look together.

MATERIALS LIST

- ○ Fabric scraps
- ○ 1 plastic headband
- ○ 3 metal shank buttons (2 different sizes)
- ○ Covered button kit
- ○ Lightweight interfacing (small piece)
- ○ Glue gun or industrial strength craft glue
- ○ Pliers

1 Using pliers, remove the metal shanks from the button backing. Cut fabric and interfacing according to the template that came with your covered button kit. Follow the manufacturer's instructions on your covered button kit. The interfacing should go between the fabric and the button. Tuck in all of the edges of the fabric and interfacing. Place the button backing on top, with the shank removed, and snap into place.

2 Cover the headband. Cut a long strip of fabric ½" (13mm) wide by the width of fabric. You may need less, but it's better to have too much than not enough. Starting with a dot of glue, wrap your headband with the fabric strip, adding a dot of glue every two wraps. Work from one side to the other. Once you've reached the end of your headband, tuck in the raw end and secure with more glue.

3 Place the three buttons off to one side of the headband with the largest one in the middle. Apply a liberal amount of glue to each button and press firmly in place. Allow glue to set for 24 hours (Fig. A).

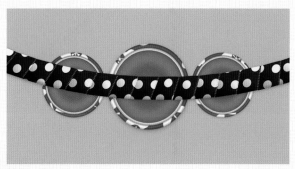

Figure A

- -

Make It Just Sew

Using a lightweight interfacing in between the fabric and the metal shank button ensures that no metal will be seen through the fabric. It makes for a much nicer, more professional-looking covered button.

Covered button kits can be found in the notions section of your local fabric store.

- -

Embellished Ruffle Shirt

The Embellished Ruffle Shirt is another way to add boutique flare to your child's handmade wardrobe. You can make this readymade embellished T-shirt coordinate with your child's favorite garments by using the same fabrics and trims. This shirt looks adorable paired with the Vintage Ruffle Capris and Shorts as well as the Banded Bloomer Shorts and Knickers, the Banded Shorts and Capris and the Twirl Skirt!

The instructions are given as ideas and inspiration, but this is a place where you can layer fabrics and trims any way you would like. Use these steps as a guideline, not as hard and fast instructions.

MATERIALS LIST

- ❍ Embellished Shirt Ruffle* (from Finishing Touches pattern pieces set)
- ❍ 1 T-shirt
- ❍ 1 fat quarter of fabric or three different coordinating fabrics
- ❍ ½–¾ yard (0.5m–0.7m) pre-gathered eyelet
- ❍ ½ yard (0.5m) rickrack trim (optional)
- ❍ Wash-A-Way Wonder Tape (optional)
- ❍ Coordinating Thread

*Pattern piece found on CD in Finishing Touches files.

1 Cut out the ruffle pattern piece. If you would like a wider ruffle (as pictured), double the width of the ruffle pattern piece. If you would prefer a more subtle ruffle, cut the pattern piece as given. For a three-layer ruffle shirt, you should probably go with the wider ruffle; for a double-ruffle shirt (one fabric ruffle, one eyelet ruffle), go with the printed ruffle pattern width.

2 Place the ruffle pieces right sides together and sew along the long curved edge. The straight edge should be left open. Clip the curves, turn right side out and press.

3 Run a row of zigzag stitches along the top raw edges of the ruffle; or if you have a serger, serge the edge. Run two rows of gathering stitches along the top raw edge of the ruffle.

4 Gather the ruffle until it is the same length as the front neckline of your shirt (different for each shirt).

5 Line up the ruffle with the neckline of the shirt using Wash-A-Way Wonder Tape or straight pins to hold the ruffle in place. Sew the ruffle in place.

6 If you are doing the wider ruffle, you can add a layer of trim on top of the first ruffle. Or you can cut the original ruffle piece and use that as your next ruffle layer.

7 Finally, add a piece of pre-gathered eyelet (cut a little longer than the width of the front curve of the neckline) on top of the ruffle. Be sure to tuck in the raw ends so they don't show. You can add rickrack on top as well, but again, make sure you turn under the two raw ends.

Make It Just Sew

Consider using pre-gathered lace or eyelet as one or all of the ruffle layers. For a more subtle look, just use one ruffle layer, or go wild and do four! Buttons would be cute on top, too. It's entirely up to you and your child's personal style.

Hair Accessory pictured with Embellished Bib Shirt
(Chapter 6) and Twirl Skirt (Chapter 1).

Vintage-Style Hair Accessory

If you've read this book from the beginning, you know that I am a big fan of rickrack. I love using it as an accent detail because it just feels vintage to me. Here is another easy accessory for you or your little lady.

This Vintage Style Hair Accessory can be attached to a headband or clip. Or consider making this into a pin for yourself so that you can coordinate with your daughter or granddaughter. Attach it to a cardigan, coat or even your purse. It's not exactly a full mother-daughter outfit, but it's always fun to make sure everyone knows that darling gal belongs with you. And a great way to do that is with a coordinating accessory!

MATERIALS LIST

- ○ Yo-Yo Templates* (large and small, from Finishing Touches pattern pieces set)
- ○ Scrap piece of fabric (enough for small circle)
- ○ Small piece of thick felt (enough for larger circle)
- ○ Rickrack (or other trim)
- ○ Pinking shears
- ○ Glue gun or industrial strength craft glue
- ○ Coordinating thread

Pattern pieces found on CD in Finishing Touches files.

1 Line up the edge of the rickrack with the raw edge of the right side of the small circle. Sew down the center of the rickrack, all the way around the circle, making sure the raw edges of the ends stick off of the edge of the circle. Press the rickrack toward the wrong side of the circle so that the edge of the rickrack shows around the edge of the circle.

2 Sew the rickrack circle to the larger felt circle. Edgestitch or topstitch around the rickrack circle, securing it to the center of the felt circle.

3 Using your pinking shears, cut around the felt to make a decorative edge. Cut very close to the edge of the rickrack all the way around. Glue the circle to a headband, clip or pin. Allow to dry for 24 hours (Fig. A).

Figure A

- -

Make It Just Sew

Add a fabric yo-yo to the center of the rickrack circle for another vintage-style variation.

- -

ADDITIONAL DESIGN IDEAS

CHAPTER 1: SMOCKS AND FROCKS

☺ Add an embroidered monogram to any bodice piece.

☺ For the Pocket Smock Top, embroider or appliqué a design onto each one of the pocket spaces prior to sewing it to the top.

☺ Embellish any bodice with buttons, ribbon or a fabric bow.

☺ Add the back pocket from the Vintage Ruffle Capris to the front of the Play Frock or Swing Smock for a different look. Or better yet, add two pockets!

☺ Sew a fabric yo-yo and hand sew it to the center-front of the round neck or bodice. Finish the center with a button.

☺ Add piping or rickrack in the seam of the collar of the Round Neck Ruffle Dress.

☺ Add piping in the seam between the top tier of the Ruffle Dress and the bodice.

☺ Use fabric-covered buttons on the back bodice to coordinate with the dress and add a little vintage touch.

CHAPTER 2: YOU BET YOUR BRITCHES

☺ Don't use the back pocket and leave the back of the capris or shorts plain.

☺ Add some trim, such as rickrack, on top of the seam between the bottom of the capris or shorts and the bottom ruffle.

☺ Find fun buttons to use on the front of the capri and shorts pockets, and on the tabs.

☺ Add some trim in the seam between the top of the capris or shorts and the front waistband.

CHAPTER 3: BABY IT'S COLD OUTSIDE

☺ Use a unique, whimsical fabric for the lining of the coat. It will be a fun surprise when your little one takes her coat on and off.

☺ Add a sweet little embroidered note in the lining of the coat. Something as simple as "I Love You" hand embroidered by Mommy or Grandma is an extra reminder of how special your child is every time she wears her handmade coat.

☺ Turn the Little Lady Coat into a button-front top. Shorten the sleeves to ¾-length, or even shorter and do not line the sleeves, but rather hem the cuff. Construct the coat from lightweight summer fabrics.

☺ Construct the coat without the collar and insert piping around the front and neck seams.

☺ Construct the coat without the pockets.

☺ If you plan to keep the sleeve cuffed, secure in place with several unique buttons.

☺ Add the neck sash and the ruffle sleeve to the long Classic Dress Coat.

CHAPTER 4: A IS FOR A-LINE

- Add piping in the armholes and neck seam.

- Add pre-gathered eyelet in the top portion of the armholes for a flutter sleeve look.

- Instead of using the loop closure in the back of the dress, insert coordinating ribbon on the right and left sides of the back slit. Tie in a bow at the back of the dress.

- Add an embroidery design to the front of the Classic A-Line Dress prior to garment construction.

- Instead of using a straight stitch for topstitching the hem of the Classic A-Line Dress, choose a fun, decorative stitch.

- Add the pockets from the Classic Dress Coat to the front of the any of the A-Line variations.

- Add a ruffle or trim down the center-front of the Classic A-Line Dress prior to garment construction.

- Add trim in the seam at the hem of the dress. Use rickrack, loopy trim, pre-gathered eyelet or any other trim that would look cute poking out of the hem of a dress.

CHAPTER 5: SUGAR, SPICE AND EVERYTHING NICE

- Add a monogram to the front of the bodice or use the interchangeable monogram from Chapter 4.

- Add piping in the armholes, around the neck and down the back of the bodice, as well as between the gathered skirt and the bodice.

- Add rickrack or piping in the seam between the sleeve binding and the puff sleeve, as well as in the seam of the Peter Pan collar.

- Layer trims around the bottom of the gathered skirt.

- Finish the bottom hem with rickrack poking out around the entire bottom of the gathered skirt or any other trim that would look cute at a hem.

- Add layered trim to the center of the bodice front, such as woven ribbon, rickrack, lace or a fabric ruffle. Do this prior to constructing the bodice.

- Construct the dress from one fabric instead of many.

- Add a double-layered fabric yo-yo to the front of the bodice.

CHAPTER 6: THE FINISHING TOUCH

- Cut off the bottom of the Embellished Bib Shirt and attach the skirt from the Sweet Dress for a quick and easy play dress.

- Personalize a store-bought T-shirt with machine- or hand-embroidery for a custom boutique look.

- Add fabric-covered buttons to hair elastics by threading the elastic through the shank of the button and looping it around to secure.

- Make a fabric ribbon out of coordinating fabric from your garment and tie in a bow as a headband or around a ponytail.

- Add ruffle elastic, gathered eyelet or lace to the top of store-bought knee socks to complete your child's look.

GLOSSARY

Appliqué: A piece of fabric sewn or applied to another piece of fabric used as an embellishment. Appliqué can be done by machine or by hand.

Baste: A stitch with a slightly longer length used to hold pattern pieces or trim in place.

Backstitch: Anchoring stitches sewn in reverse at the beginning and the end of a seam.

Casing: A long, narrow tube opening in fabric usually used to hold ribbon, elastic or drawstring in place.

Edgestitching: Similar to topstitching, but sewn ⅛" (3mm) from the edge of the seam.

Gathering Stitch: *See Techniques section.*

Fat Quarter: A fat quarter is a ¼ yard (0.2m) of fabric, cut 18" (46cm) wide by 22" (56cm) long.

Hem: The finished edge of a garment.

Interfacing: An extra piece of fabric used to give fabric more body, weight and substance. Interfacing comes in many different forms, such as fusible, double-sided fusible, sew-in, and can be woven and nonwoven.

Press Seam Allowances: Once you have sewn a seam, you will need to press it. Press the seam flat to set the stitches and then press the seam open. In quilting, you would press the seam to one side, but for the purposes of the patterns in this book, you will press the seams open (away from the seam).

Right Side of Fabric: The side of the fabric that will be visible on the exterior of the garment. If you are using quilting-weight cotton, it is the side with the print on it (the opposite side will typically be more white). Occasionally, you will find a fabric, such as soft wool, that can be used on either side.

Satin Stitch: A zigzag stitch set at a very short stitch length, often used in appliqué. You can also use satin stitches to finish the edge of fabric. I prefer to use embroidery thread for satin stitching.

Seam Allowance: The amount of fabric between the edge of the fabric and the stitching. All patterns included in this book have a ½" (13mm) seam allowance included, unless otherwise noted.

Selvage: The two lengthwise, finished edges of the fabric that run down both sides are called the selvage. The selvages are woven differently from the main fabric and should be removed prior to sewing due to their different shrinkage rate.

Topstitching: A straight line of stitches ¼" (6mm) from the edge of the seam or fabric. It is often used as a decorative detail and helps the edges to lay flat, which adds a more finished look to a garment.

Wrong Side of Fabric: The side of the fabric that will not be seen on the outside of the garment. The wrong side is typically the nonprinted side of the fabric. In the case where it is difficult to tell the right or wrong side, you can make the choice of which side you would like to use.

ACKNOWLEDGMENTS

First and foremost, I'd like to thank my family for all of their love and support. Thank you for helping me turn my dream into a reality. I love you all!

To my husband, Brett, thank you for all those weekends you spent flying solo playing Mr. Mom to our kids so I could work on this book. I could not ask for a better father for our children and a more supportive husband. The Cottage Mama would not be possible without you.

To my children, you are my inspiration. You are the reason why I do all that I do. Thank you for loving me unconditionally. Thank you for loving fabric almost as much as I do, and thank you for your excitement when you put on a garment made by Mommy. Savannah and Matilda, your beauty shines through the photographs in this book, and you will always be my sweet little girls.

To my mom, I don't even have the proper words to express what you mean to me. Never in my life did you ever let me think that my dreams were not a possibility. You have always taught me to shoot for the stars and that anything is possible. Thank you for being such a rock in my life. You are an incredible mother and an amazing best friend. I love you from here to the moon and back again.

To my photographer and friend, Amy Tripple (www.amytripplephotography.com), thank you for capturing the sweet essence of girlhood in this book. You were truly a joy to watch working with all of the little girls that appear in the pages of this book. Your work is fresh and absolutely lovely. But what is even more impressive is your beautiful spirit inside and out. This book would not be what it is without you.

A big thank you to my editors and all the fabulous folks at F+W Media, Inc. Thank you to Kelly Biscopink for seeing potential in my work and believing it would make a good book. It has been a pleasure working with a publisher that allows its authors so much creative freedom. Thank you, from the bottom of my heart, for this opportunity.

To my amazing sewing machine sponsor, Baby Lock Sewing and Embroidery Machines (www.babylock.com), thank you so much for providing me with the most gorgeous sewing machine (Baby Lock Unity) and serger (Baby Lock Evolution) I have ever used in my entire life. It was definitely "love at first stitch." Every single garment in this book was sewn on a Baby Lock machine, and I am very thankful to be working with such a high-quality company.

A big thank you to all of the fabric manufacturers that provided fabric for this book: Fabric Finders (www.fabricfindersinc.com), Riley Blake Designs (www.rileyblakedesigns.com), Michael Miller Fabrics (www.michaelmillerfabrics.com), Windham Fabrics (www.windhamfabrics.com) and Timeless Treasures (www.ttfabrics.com).

To Isabelle, thank you so much for your help and pattern expertise. So glad we got to work on this project together! You are such a wealth of knowledge, and I truly appreciate your guidance through the last several years working together. Here's to many more!

Thank you to all of the little girls who appear in this book: Savannah, Matilda, Kate, Kenzie, Emily, Isadora, Abby, Caleigh, Piper, Madeleine, Sophia and Annie. A big thanks to you and your parents for taking time out of your lives to make it to photo shoots and being part of this project. You girls bring these clothes to life.

Thank you to Livie and Luca (www.livieandluca.com) for providing the adorable shoes seen on the darling little girls throughout the book.

Many of the lovely trims used are from Renaissance Ribbons (renaissanceribbons.com) and Farmhouse Fabrics (www.farmhousefabrics.com).

And last, but certainly not least, thank you to all of the amazing The Cottage Mama blog readers and fans. Your kind, sweet words and support have given me the drive to work as hard as I do and make all of this happen. I hope you all love this book as much as I do; I thought of you all every step of the way. My most sincere thanks.

Sew Classic Clothes for Girls. Copyright © 2013 by Lindsay Wilkes. Manufactured in China. All rights reserved. The patterns and drawings in this book are for the personal use of the reader. By permission of the author and publisher, they may be either hand-traced or photocopied to make single copies, but under no circumstances may they be resold or republished. It is permissible for the purchaser to create the designs contained herein and sell them at fairs, bazaars and craft shows. No other part of this book may be reproduced in any form or by any electronic or mechanical means including information storage and retrieval systems without permission in writing from the publisher, except by a reviewer who may quote brief passages in a review. Published by KP Craft, an imprint of F+W Media, Inc., 10150 Carver Road, Blue Ash, Ohio 45242. (800) 289-0963. First Edition.

www.fwmedia.com

17 16 15 14 13   5 4 3 2 1

DISTRIBUTED IN CANADA BY FRASER DIRECT
100 Armstrong Avenue
Georgetown, ON, Canada L7G 5S4
Tel: (905) 877-4411

DISTRIBUTED IN THE U.K. AND EUROPE BY F+W MEDIA INTERNATIONAL
Brunel House, Newton Abbot, Devon, TQ12 4PU, England
Tel: (+44) 1626 323200, Fax: (+44) 1626 323319
Email: postmaster@davidandcharles.co.uk

DISTRIBUTED IN AUSTRALIA BY CAPRICORN LINK
P.O. Box 704, S. Windsor NSW, 2756 Australia
Tel: (02) 4577-3555

SRN: U2256
ISBN-13: 978-1-4402-3518-4

Layout Editor: Layne Vanover
Content Editor: Kelly Biscopink
Designer: Michelle Thompson
Illustrator: Lindsay Quinter
Pattern and Layout Illustrator: Isabelle M. Lott
Production Coordinator: Greg Nock

Metric Conversion Chart

To convert	to	multiply by
Inches	Centimeters	2.54
Centimeters	Inches	0.4
Feet	Centimeters	30.5
Centimeters	Feet	0.03
Yards	Meters	0.9
Meters	Yards	1.1

INDEX

MORE CLASSIC SEWING BOOKS!

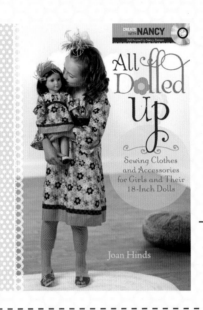

Stitch Savvy

BY DEBORAH MOEBES

In *Stitch Savvy,* customize your sewing education with 5 sewing tracks (home décor, handbags, kids' items, quilting and clothing). Each track features 5 projects that start simple and gradually increase in difficulty to build up your sewing skills. Cross-referenced techniques allow you to skip around and explore certain skills. (You loved the box pleats in the Sashiko curtains? Check out the A-line skirt with the peek-a-boo pleat!) Get savvy, one stitch at a time.

All Dolled Up

BY JOAN HINDS

A girl and her doll are fast friends indeed. Add in coordinating outfits, and nothing could be cuter! Make adorable coordinating outfits for the girl in your life and the doll in hers with the help of *All Dolled Up.* From flowered party dresses, summer tops and capri pants to fleece vests and messenger bags, these projects provide easy, fun and fashionable outfits for every season and time of day.

More Sewing with Whimsy

BY KARI MECCA

More Sewing with Whimsy is a fanciful treat in children's sewing and embellishing. Beginning with a classic pattern based on a simple silhouette, each chapter guides the sewing enthusiast along a path of originality filled with gorgeous trims and timeless techniques. Featuring step-by-step directions and a simple construction approach, Kari Mecca's one-of-a-kind projects and ideas range from fun and funky to sweet and sassy that will be just right for the little gal in your life.

These and other fine KP Craft titles are available at your local craft retailer, bookstore or online supplier, or visit our website at Store.MarthaPullen.com.

 fwcraft

 @fwcraft